SEVEN SKILLS FOR SCHOOL SUCCESS

by Pam Schiller

Acknowledgments

Dedication

To Dr. Harry Chugani and Dr. Bruce Perry, who continue to produce scientific evidence supporting the crucial role that early interactions and experiences play in developing social and emotional intelligence.

To Daniel Goleman, who elegantly spreads the news!

To sweet baby Audrey, who is living proof that loving parents who are fully present make a significant difference.

Additional Gryphon House Books Written by Pam Schiller

The Complete Resource Book for Infants: Over 700 Experiences for Children From Birth to 18 Months

The Complete Resource Book for Toddlers and Twos: Over 2000 Experiences and Ideas

Creating Readers: Over 1000 Games, Activities, Tongue Twisters, Fingerplays, Songs, and Stories to Get Children Excited About Reading

The Complete Resource Book: An Early Childhood Curriculum, with Kay Hastings

The Complete Book of Rhymes, Songs, Poems, Fingerplays, and Chants, with Jackie Silberg

The Complete Book of Activities, Games, Stories, Props, Recipes, and Dances, with Jackie Silberg

The Bilingual Book of Rhymes, Songs, Stories, and Fingerplays, with Rafael Lara-Alecio and Beverly J. Irby

Start Smart: Building Brain Power in the Early Years

The Practical Guide to Quality Child Care, with Patricia Carter Dyke

The Values Book, with Tamera Bryant

Count on Math: Activities With Small Hands and Lively Minds, with Lynne Peterson

Where Is Thumbkin?, with Thomas Moore

The Instant Curriculum, Revised, with Joan Rosanno

Do You Know the Muffin Man? with Thomas Moore

SOCIAL & EMOTIONAL INTELLIGENCE

Seven Skills
for School
Success

Activities to Develop
Social & Emotional
Intelligence in
Young Children

Pam Schiller

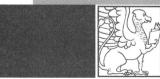

gryphon house, inc.
Beltsville, MD, USA

Seven Skills for School Success

by Pam Schiller

© 2009 Pam Schiller

Published by Gryphon House, Inc.

PO Box 207, Beltsville, MD 20704

800.638.0928; 301.595.9500; 301.595.0051 (fax)

Visit us on the web at www.gryphonhouse.com

Cover Art: Straight Shots Product Photography, Ellicott City, MD.

Library of Congress Cataloging-in-Publication Information

Schiller, Pamela Byrne.

  Seven skills for school success / by Pam Schiller.

    p. cm.

  ISBN 978-0-87659-071-3

  1. Readiness for school. 2. Social learning. 3. Child development. 4. Success. I. Title.

  LB1132.S315 2009

  372.21--dc22

                          2009005486

Bulk purchase

Gryphon House books are available for special premiums and sales promotions as well as for fund-raising use. Special editions or book excerpts also can be created to specification. For details, contact the Director of Marketing at Gryphon House.

Disclaimer

Gryphon House, Inc. and the author cannot be held responsible for damage, mishap, or injury incurred during the use of or because of activities in this book. Appropriate and reasonable caution and adult supervision of children involved in activities and corresponding to the age and capability of each child involved is recommended at all times. Do not leave children unattended at any time. Observe safety and caution at all times.

Table of Contents

SEVEN SKILLS FOR SCHOOL SUCCESS

Introduction

All children need social and emotional skills so they can learn and be successful in school and in life. To be successful academically, children need to learn how to control their emotions and how to work in groups; these skills are necessary to thrive in school or any other learning situation. Children who can control their impulses and behaviors are much better prepared to listen and learn.

Society values an individual's cognitive capabilities; yet many people do not stop to consider how individuals actually develop these skills. We want children to be successful in school, and, generally, good grades are measures of that success. We may assume that good grades are the result of superior cognitive abilities. However, children need to learn to pay attention and listen so they can develop the thinking skills necessary to become successful students. Paying attention and listening require children to control impulses, delay gratification, and focus on a task. All of these are related to social and emotional development.

For example, when an individual is a gifted athlete, we may believe that, beyond her physical talents, it is her cognitive abilities that make her exceptional. This type of thinking is "putting the cart before the horse." It is more likely that she has used her social and emotional skills—her ability to control her impulses and delay gratification—to focus on practicing the physical and mental skills necessary to become an exceptional player.

New findings from neurological science support the crucial role social and emotional development play in learning. Researchers (Sousa, 2005; Goleman, 2006) suggest that cognitive and physical potential is optimized only when an individual's brain is adequately wired in the areas of social and emotional intelligence.

This book reviews some of the more recent research findings related to social and emotional development and suggests strategies for applying this important research as you work with children. In addition, it explores important characteristics of social and emotional intelligence and offers easy-to-implement activities to help children develop these characteristics to the fullest.

WHAT IS SOCIAL INTELLIGENCE?

Social intelligence covers the broad range of skills people use to relate to, play with, learn from, and teach others. Social skills are important for survival and for a good life.

Individuals who are socially intelligent are able to:
- Assess the feelings of others;
- Relate to the feelings, motives, and concerns of others;
- Read and respond to social cues; and
- Negotiate and resolve conflicts.

A group of children are playing Keep Away. Hunter is watching from the sidelines. Each time the ball comes close to him, he makes a feeble attempt to intercept it. Amanda notices that Hunter appears interested in the game. When the ball comes her way, she catches it and announces to the group, "Hey, Hunter wants to play with us. Come on, Hunter, you can be on my team."

Amanda exhibits a high level of social intelligence. She is attuned to the feelings of others. She notices Hunter on the sidelines watching. She reads social cues. Hunter's attempt to intercept the ball registers with Amanda as a sign that Hunter would like to play. Amanda responds by waiting for an appropriate time to stop the game. She helps Hunter join, and she helps her teammates become aware of the situation.

WHAT IS EMOTIONAL INTELLIGENCE?

Healthy emotions allow people to express and constructively manage the full range of human feelings, to postpone gratification, to find constructive outlets for negative emotions, and to understand and appreciate how others feel. Healthy emotions lead to self-satisfaction and joy.

Individuals who are emotionally intelligent are able to:
- Identify and label feelings,
- Express feelings,
- Assess the intensity of feelings,
- Manage feelings,
- Delay gratification,
- Control impulses,
- Know the difference between feeling and actions, and
- Manage stress.

> *A group of children are playing Red Rover at a birthday party. John wants to play with them. He has been watching the other children play. Several times, he tells the children that he would like to play. Heather stops playing, but before she has a chance to tell John he can take her place, Michael takes her place. John sees his opportunity is gone. He tells Michael that he was waiting and was the next in line to play. Michael says, "Too bad!" John starts to cry. Daniel says, "John, you can play in my place. I am going inside to play with Heather."*

What happened here? Who demonstrates competency in the area of emotional intelligence? What about John? He waits patiently, he communicates his desires, he tries to negotiate with Michael, and he refrains from kicking or hitting Michael. These are all important building blocks of emotional intelligence. His tears are his way of communicating his frustration and stress. He handles himself well for a four-year-old. He demonstrates intentionality, effective communication skills, an ability to control his impulses, and the ability to wait. Instead of tears, he could have taken his frustration out on Michael.

Daniel also shows a high level of emotional intelligence and social intelligence. He demonstrates empathy for John and is willing to move on to another activity to allow John to have a turn.

There is not much information about Michael in the scenario, but he likely has not mastered empathy yet.

SOCIAL AND EMOTIONAL INTELLIGENCE ARE INTERDEPENDENT

Emotional intelligence is the understanding and managing of one's feelings and emotions. Social intelligence is the understanding and managing of oneself in group situations. The two are interdependent. Most often a child will learn to understand and manage himself before he becomes skilled at understanding and managing himself in the company of others. However, children also learn about themselves by watching and interacting with others. The chart below shows how the skills for social and emotional intelligence support each other.

Emotional Intelligence	Social Intelligence
Self-awareness Understands feelings Knows the difference between feelings and actions	**Social awareness** Assesses the feeling of others Reads social cues Relates to the feelings, motives, and concerns of others Is attuned to the feelings, motives, and concerns of others
Self-management Exercises feelings Manages feelings Controls impulses Communicates feelings Manages stress	**Relationship management** Negotiates and resolves conflicts Responds to the feelings, motives, and concerns of others Works cooperatively with others Communicates effectively with others Demonstrates strategies for entering group play

WHAT BRAIN RESEARCH SAYS ABOUT SOCIAL AND EMOTIONAL INTELLIGENCE

Wiring the Foundation for Brain Power

The primary task of the brain during early childhood is to connect brain cells (neurons). Every neuron has an axon, which sends information out to other neurons, and several dendrites, which receive information from the other cells. As axons hook up with dendrites, trillions of connections, called synapses, are formed. Everything we learn is stored in communities of neurons. We have neurological communities assigned to operate our motor, cognitive, and language capabilities, as well as our social and emotional capabilities.

Experience forges the connections, and repetition strengthens the forged connections for all areas of development. The first time an experience is encountered, neurons connect. When the experience is revisited or repeated, the information travels over the established circuitry and, in doing so, strengthens the connections. In neurological terms, the axons become more highly myelinated. When the axons within the community are fully myelinated, information is able to travel at an incredible rate of 200 mps (miles per second) over the brain's circuitry (Sousa, 2005). Think about the circuitry like paths through the wilderness—those paths that are used the most become highways and those that are not used tend to fade away.

Social and emotional wiring differ from cognitive and physical wiring in that they are uniquely dependent on human interactions (Goleman, 2007). We must interact socially with others in order to forge social networks in the brain. Our ability to relate to others comes from the application of what we have learned from those early interactions to the broader world. Emotional wiring is laid down during the first few years of life as children interact with their parents and caregivers and determine that they are able to get their needs met. The ability to control emotions and manage impulses depends on the wiring of this trust.

> The quality and quantity of social and emotional experiences will affect the outcome of social intelligence and emotional intelligence (Goleman, 2007).

The Social and Emotional Brain

The social brain is the sum of the neural mechanisms that orchestrate our interactions as well as our thoughts and feelings about people and our relationships. Social wiring requires face-to-face, voice-to-voice, and skin-to-skin contact with others.

The emotional brain is the sum of the neural mechanisms that orchestrate and manage our emotions and our impulses. Positive emotional wiring requires confidence that we are safe.

Developmental Timetables

There are fertile times when the brain is able to wire specific skills at an optimum level. These fertile times are called "windows of opportunity." The windows are scientific; they are open from birth to puberty. The open windows of opportunity are the same for all children, no matter where on the planet they are born, no matter the conditions under which they are born, no matter whether they are premature, developmentally delayed, or typically developing.

Social and emotional intelligence foundations are wired during the first 48 months of life. Positive experiences during open (fertile) windows result in positive outcomes. Negative experiences during open windows result in negative outcomes. For example, in terms of emotional intelligence, an infant wires trust during the first 14 months of life. If he cries and someone comes to help him, he will wire for trust; if no one comes to his aid, he will wire for lack of trust (Ramey & Ramey, 1999). If he is hungry and someone feeds him, he learns to trust, but if no one feeds him, he learns not to trust. It is as simple as that.

When positive experiences are offered according to the timetable provided in the following chart, Windows of Opportunity, wiring will occur at an optimum level. The brain is fertile all through the early years and up to puberty, so the skills listed within each window are technically able to wire during that time. However, optimum wiring occurs when positive experiences occur within the designated window.

Windows of Opportunity

Window	Wiring Opportunity	Greatest Enhancement

Social Intelligence
    Attachment
    Independence
    Cooperation
	0–48 months
	0–12 months
	18–36 months
	24–48 months
		4 years to puberty

Emotional Intelligence
    Trust
    Impulse Control
	0–48 months
	0–14 months
	16–48 months
		4 years to puberty

Motor Development	0–24 months	2 years to puberty
Vision	0–24 months	2 years to puberty

Thinking Skills
    Cause and Effect
    Problem Solving
	0–48 months
	0–16 months
	16–48 months
		4 years to puberty

Window	Wiring Opportunity	Greatest Enhancement
Reading Foundation Skills*	0–24 months	2–7 years
Early Sounds	4–8 months	8 months to puberty
Vocabulary	0–24 months	2–5 years

* Two reliable predictors of reading success are sound discrimination and the size of the individual's vocabulary.

Use the Windows of Opportunity chart as a guide when planning social and emotional experiences for children. The windows of opportunity provide a framework for what is best for children. For the greatest enhancement, offer positive experiences during fertile (open) windows and provide numerous opportunities for repetition, which should follow as closely as possible to new experiences.

Spindle Cells

At birth, there are 100 trillion neurons waiting to be wired. The brain is an amazingly unfinished organ at birth. Connections are forged as children encounter experiences in the world, and they are reinforced with subsequent repetitions of the experience. This becomes the neural circuitry that will lay the foundation for children's lifelong learning. Some of the 100 trillion neurons waiting to be connected are specifically assigned to wire for social and emotional intelligence.

Social wiring is forged by social experiences. Spindle cells, named after their long, spindle-shaped bodies, are the cells that are credited with allowing us to feel love and to suffer emotionally (Goleman, 2007). These cells occur in parts of the human brain that are thought to be responsible for social orchestration (interactions). They are responsible for empathy, speech, intuition about the feelings of others, and snap judgments.

Spindle cells make us socially aware and sensitive. Scientists believe that spindle cells create our interpersonal intelligence. Humans, some species of apes, and humpback whales are the only animals with spindle cells. Spindle cells position themselves in the brain during the first four months of life. How prolific they are depends on factors such as stress (for worse) and loving atmosphere (for the better).

Mirror Neurons

Mirror neurons are also related to our social and emotional skills. They form during the first few years of life as we watch others. Mirror neurons make emotions contagious. They are the neurons that allow babies to smile after only a few short weeks of experiencing human interactions.

Mirror neurons help us sense the intentions of others and are invaluable when it comes to gathering social information. Mirror neurons fire as we watch others. They are firing when we smile back at someone who smiles at us. They are firing when one crying baby makes other babies begin to cry. Scientists claim that the more active a person's mirror neuron system is, the stronger the capability for empathy.

Effects of Stress

Emotional trauma can have a negative impact on early development. Children who are stressed carry a high level of cortisol (the stress hormone) in their bloodstreams. High levels of cortisol cause adults to have "fuzzy" thinking, but for young children it is far more damaging. When cortisol washes over the newly formed neurological connections of young children, it can literally wash away some of those fragile new connections—leaving children struggling to build the necessary foundation for lifetime learning (Families and Work Institute, 1996).

Emotional trauma also interferes with the brain's ability to use rational thought to decode our emotions. It over-sensitizes us to stress and causes us to over-react to situations.

Do young children have stress? Yes! Although the causes of their stress may be invisible to most adults, they often carry a high level of stress. What causes stress in children? They are struggling to meet developmental milestones: learning to communicate, to walk, to interact, to trust, to sustain emotional balance, and to understand their world. One of the greatest stressors for young children is building rapport with those involved in their daily lives. For example, when a child's teacher leaves and a new one takes her place, it may take this child a long time to make the adjustment to someone new. During this period of time, the child will encounter stress with each interaction.

In the middle of the last century, Romania was an impoverished country where families could not afford to have children because they were too poor to keep food on the table.

The Czar of Romania at that time was concerned that without a population, one day there would be no more Romania. So he made a law that each woman within child-bearing age had to have at least 4 children, and those who did not comply had to pay a heavy tax.

Reluctantly, the families in Romania began to have more children. However, they could not provide for these children because of their poverty.

The government stepped in and took over the care of these children and placed them in large orphanages. The orphanages were all the same—a central tower with four wings, three stories high—40 children on each wing with 1 caretaker for each wing.

In these orphanages, conditions were inadequate. The color was drab and there were no toys or books. The caretakers could not possibly take care of all the children, so bottles were propped up and diapers were changed only when absolutely necessary. Many of the children remained in their cribs day and night, like animals in cages. Nutrition was also poor and many became malnourished.

Importantly, little or no emotional or social interaction occurred between the children and caregivers or other adults. No one read to them, no one played with them or held them, and no one showed affection to these unfortunate children. Yet, healthy social interaction early in life is crucial to normal emotional development.

This was convincingly demonstrated in experiments on newborn monkeys performed by Dr. Harry Harlow in the 1960s. Dr. Harlow reared newborn monkeys in complete isolation and found that if the period of isolation exceeded 8 months, the young monkeys were not accepted into colonies because of their abnormal and delinquent behavior. Monkeys reach puberty between 3 and 4 years, so 8 months was long before puberty.

Dr. Harry T. Chugani, a pediatric neurologist, and Dr. Michael E. Behen, a pediatric neuropsychologist, from Wayne State University, have studied the effects of early socio-emotional deprivation on young children for a number of years. They were familiar with the Harlow experiments and wanted to study effects of deprivation on the brain. The Romanian orphans became part of their research. Drs. Chugani and Behen have followed these children from the time they arrived as adopted orphans and have performed a variety of neuroimaging studies to determine the effects of early socio-emotional deprivation on brain function and connectivity. They also performed behavioral assessments on the children.

Drs. Chugani and Behen found that most of these children had a difficult time overcoming the effects of their early deprivation. They had impulsive behaviors, attention deficits, and attachment disorders. Like in the Harlow monkeys, there seemed to be a critical period, in that children who were adopted prior to 18 months of age fared better than those who were adopted later. Indeed, several siblings adopted by the same foster parents were noted to have different outcomes, with the younger ones doing better because they had spent less time in the orphanage and had been placed in caring environments sooner.

Dr. Chugani and his team used advanced brain imaging techniques, including PET (positron emission tomography) and DTI (diffusion tensor imaging, an advanced MRI technique that can look at tracts or connections in the brain), to study these children. They found that certain areas of the brain, called limbic regions, were functioning poorly and were abnormally connected to each other. In normal people, these same regions are known to be involved in emotional and social skills. Dr. Chugani concluded that if the infant does not use certain brain areas and connections that are waiting for attachment and bonding, then these areas fail to stabilize or "hard wire," leading to disturbances in the behavior of these children as they grow up. The first 18–24 months are crucial for this hard wiring to occur properly.

This story is reprinted with the permission of Dr. Harry T. Chugani.

Sleep Deprivation

Many children are sleeping one to two hours less per night than their brains need for healthy growth (Gurian, 2007). Sleep deprivation denies the brain the necessary time for processing, and it denies body cells the necessary time for regenerating. Sleep deprivation in children has another negative effect—it causes antisocial behavior. Children who are tired whine and fuss. They are uninterested in participating in social activities. Researchers say that children who are sleep-deprived are more likely to do poorly in school and are prone to become substance abusers (Gurian, 2007).

Young children are wiring their brains for future use based on the experiences they encounter each day. If those experiences are antisocial in nature, then the wiring that is forged will be reinforced for antisocial behavior. Children need 8–10 hours of sleep each day. Infants and toddlers require an even greater number of hours of sleep.

Impact of Television and Computers on Social Intelligence

Both the computer and the television are antisocial mechanisms. Neither requires interpersonal interactions. Instead, both seduce children into solitary play.

During the first year of life, an infant's brain grows its particular set of necessary connections through reciprocal relationships. (See mirror neurons and spindle cells, pages 15 and 16). Synapses form through interactions with people. Babies need to be touched, spoken to, and listened to. Television and other screen stimulants can derail this brain development (Gurian, 2007; Jensen, 2005). The American Medical Association and every other medical association that has studied the impact of television on early brain development recommend avoiding screen time for children younger than two.

In *Endangered Minds,* Dr. Jane Healy speaks to the need for children to be active participants in the wiring of their brains. She says, "A 'good' brain for learning develops strong and widespread neural highways that can quickly and efficiently assign different aspects of a task to the most efficient system…. Such efficiency is developed only by active practice in thinking and learning, which, in turn, builds increasingly stronger connections."

Dr. Healy goes on to say that excessive television viewing may affect the development of strong and widespread neural networks because it is primarily a passive activity that not only fails to offer opportunity for wiring but at the same time prohibits wiring because it takes the place of active exploration.

A growing suspicion among brain researchers is that computers have the same effect. They deprive children of activities specifically needed to build strong brain connections.

SEVEN KEY ELEMENTS FOR SCHOOL SUCCESS

Over the past two decades, brain research has highlighted the preschool years as a critical transition point in childhood development; it has also highlighted the importance of early experiences to promote optimum wiring in all areas of development: social, emotional, motor, cognitive, and language.

What teachers have known for decades, the research community has confirmed: an inextricable link exists between social-emotional competence and school readiness. In their review of the literature on social and emotional intelligence, Mitchell and Glossop (2005) concluded that:

> Social and emotional intelligence is a crucial determinant of a child's "readiness to learn." That readiness depends on seven key elements, which the research has defined as:
> * Confidence
> * Curiosity
> * Intentionality
> * Self-control
> * Relatedness
> * Capacity to communicate
> * Cooperativeness

Although research clearly identifies these seven characteristics as critical for school success, the focus continues to be on early academic training. Yet, a child's readiness for school is not measured by how many letters of the alphabet he knows or how high she can count. It is not contingent on early reading or math ability. It depends on the less-tangible criteria related to social and emotional intelligence. Daniel Goleman, in *Social Intelligence*, says,

> *Those who say that social intelligence amounts to little more than general intelligence applied to social situations might do better to reason the other way around: to consider that general intelligence is merely a derivative of social intelligence, albeit one our culture has come to value.*

Focusing on helping children develop each of the seven key elements will enhance their social and emotional intelligence and will help those children achieve their full potential as individuals and as members of society.

TEACHING FOR LEARNING

1. Model

Do you remember the old saying, "a picture is worth a thousand words"? Well, when it comes to teaching children, this is profoundly true. Children are always watching us; everything we do teaches a lesson. For example, if we want our children to be cooperative, confident, and intentional, then we must demonstrate those behaviors to them in all that we do—not just when it suits us.

Demonstrating the characteristics we want children to acquire is not a part-time job. Children are pragmatic, fairly black-and-white in their thinking. The concept of "extenuating circumstances" is beyond their comprehension. Young children have not yet formed an understanding of discretion or the ability to look at a situation from several points of view.

To children, you are the most important people in the world. Because they want to grow up just like you, they imitate and take to heart all that you do. This is a powerful position; enjoy it and use it wisely because all too soon that power will shift from you to their peers. If you have provided a strong foundation, the key components that make up children's social and emotional intelligence will stay with them even through the spirit-shaking teenage years.

2. Discuss

In our busy, day-to-day world, it is easy to forget why discussing things is important. It is often easier to say something and move on or to take care of a crisis by yourself. A good example of how to use discussion is when it is time to clean up. A discussion might go like this:

Why do you think it is important to clean up the toys?
Because the room needs to be neat!
Yes, it is nice for the room to be neat and tidy. What might happen if the toys are left on the floor?
Someone might step on them and break them.
Yes, they might break or someone might trip on a toy and get hurt. Have you ever tripped on something that was left out on the floor?

I did. I fell down when I stepped on a shoe.

The toys might also get lost.

That's right. If we leave the toys scattered on the table or on the floor, some of them might get lost. I have put eight blocks on the floor. Will you pick them up and put them away?

By myself?

Do you want some help?

Yes.

Why?

Because it is too many blocks for just me.

Oh, you mean if more people help, the work will be easier?

Yes, and faster.

When everyone helps clean up, the work is finished more quickly. When everyone helps clean up, the work is divided so each person has less to do.

What comes after clean-up time?

When you see children sharing, being responsible, showing empathy, practicing persistence, or other positive traits, acknowledge them with specific feedback.

Notice that the discussion is short and that a concrete example is used. You don't want to overdo discussion because children will lose interest. The concrete example of the blocks helps children see the benefits of cooperative effort in cleaning up.

Children's books provide an intriguing source of discussion material. The plots can often serve as a springboard for a discussion that will increase children's understanding and expand their thinking.

3. Practice

Children need opportunities to practice skills. Practice is important when learning something new. It helps children make sense of what they are learning. The more relevant the practice is to children's lives, the more meaningful it is and, therefore, the easier it is to master the task at hand. Practice strengthens brain connections associated with new skills, which will lead to faster retrieval of information and knowledge. For practice to be effective, children need to receive feedback from you and to do their own self-evaluation. Feedback helps children learn things correctly. If they are practicing something the wrong way they are not achieving their goals.

4. Acknowledge

When you see children sharing, being responsible, showing empathy, practicing persistence, or other positive traits, acknowledge them with specific feedback. For example, you might say, "Alicia, I noticed you helping Abby finish the puzzle. It sure is easier when two people work together, isn't it?"

While it is important to encourage children, avoid offering external rewards like stickers, allowances, candy, and so on. Ultimately, you want children to be rewarded by the internal joy they experience when they solve a problem or finish a project they have worked on diligently.

5. Reflect

One of the most disheartening by-products of our fast-paced lifestyles is the lack of time for reflection. Yet, we are often reminded of how important taking time to examine progress is to the achievement of goals. As children practice new skills, remember how important it is to provide feedback and support and to encourage them to think about how they feel about their progress.

SEVEN SKILLS FOR SCHOOL SUCCESS

Confidence

1

WHAT IS CONFIDENCE?

A feeling of emotional security that results from faith in oneself. It is a firm belief in one's powers, abilities, or capacities. (Adapted from Webster's II New College Dictionary)

Confident children meet challenges with optimism and persistence. They are able to make decisions and choices without the influence of adults or peers.

A Child Shows Confidence When...	A Confident Child Understands These Words...	
● He presents himself effectively.	able	independent
● She recognizes her ability to affect outcomes.	attitude	obstacles
● He identifies problems and seeks solutions.	can	optimistic
● She shows persistence and determination.	capable	persistent
● He demonstrates a positive attitude.	challenges	problem-solving
● She listens attentively.	confidence	proud
● He seeks adult help when needed.	confident	self
	courage	solve
	determined	success
	failure	

WHY CONFIDENCE MATTERS

Confidence develops over time. It is an attitude that reflects a positive and realistic perception of ourselves and our abilities. Confidence is learned, not inherited, and it develops from the inside out. Each of us builds our own level of confidence, layer by layer, from the experiences we encounter and how we manage these experiences. Our confidence is also influenced by the reactions of those around us. Gender, social class, religion, and culture each contribute to feelings of self-worth and confidence.

You play a major role in developing children's confidence. Your reactions tell children if you approve or disapprove of their efforts, which in turn influence their self-evaluation. If you encourage children's problem-solving and applaud their efforts, not just their successes, you promote confidence. When children solve child-size problems, they gradually learn that they do not need to fear failure and that they gain a great deal by trying.

> "If I have the belief that I can do it, I shall surely acquire the capacity to do it even if I may not have it at the beginning."
> —Mahatma Gandhi

Criticism and blame diminish confidence. Verbal and physical abuse damage children's feelings of emotional security and faith in themselves. In addition, children are self-centered, which may cause them to blame themselves for things they actually play no role in, such as a divorce or death of a loved one.

Children learn about the world and their place in it by watching the people around them. If you desire a child to be confident, you must model that behavior. Self-confident people are optimistic, independent, proud of their efforts, able to handle criticism, and emotionally mature. Self-confident people inspire self-confidence in others.

Self-confident children understand that life is full of ups and downs. They understand that when they encounter obstacles sometimes they will succeed and sometimes they will fail in overcoming them. They are realists, not perfectionists. If children always fail, they will lose the validation they need to develop confidence. If they always succeed, they will not know how to react to failure. Real confidence requires an understanding of the possibility of failure while still pursuing a solution. Confident people have a deep, realistic faith in their abilities.

WHAT THE RESEARCH SAYS
● External reward inhibits internal motivation.
● Self-efficacy (well-defined confidence) is a byproduct of problem solving.
(Bandura, 2000; Jensen, 2005)

WHAT YOU CAN DO TO BOOST A CHILD'S CONFIDENCE SKILLS

Model Confidence

- **Describe one of your challenges.** When something occurs during the course of your day that seems difficult, say, "Hmm, it is going to be difficult to organize this toy shelf, but I bet I can do it. I'm sure going to try." Celebrate by saying, "I did it!" when you accomplish your goal.

- **Talk about the pros and cons of a solution.** When you are faced with a problem, talk about it. Point out your options and discuss why you are selecting a certain option. For example, if you are trying to figure out the best place to put a new sandbox, you might describe each possible spot you are considering. Discuss the pros and cons of each location. For example, one spot is shady most of the day, but another spot is far enough away from the door to allow sand to drop off. Ask the child to think of additional pros and cons and even perhaps another location. When you make a decision, explain the rationale for your choice.

Talk About Confidence

- **Define it.** Encourage the child to believe she can succeed even if she has to try several times. Describe some familiar people or characters who are confident; for example, the Itsy Bitsy Spider, the little blue engine in *The Little Engine That Could,* and the Little Red Hen.

- **Encourage children to try something new.** Ask the child how she feels when she learns something new, such as how to walk on the balance beam, skip, or turn a somersault. Point out that every time she conquers something new she is learning and problem solving. This will help build her confidence.

- **Create an "I Did It" spot.** When a child accomplishes a difficult task, ask her to draw a picture about the experience and help her write a sentence or two about how the accomplishment made her feel. Create an "I Did It" spot on the wall for the pictures. Visit this spot often and talk about the pictures.

● **Read books.** The following books are wonderful stories about being confident or finding the confidence to do difficult things. Talk about the role of confidence in the stories you choose to read. For example, read *Amazing Grace* by Mary Hoffman. Ask questions. *How did Grace become confident? How do you know she wasn't confident at the beginning of the story?*

A Chair for My Mother by Vera Williams
Amazing Grace by Mary Hoffman
Ant Attack! by Anne James
Benjamin Dilley's Thirsty Camel by Jolly Roger Bradfield
Caps for Sale by Esphyr Slobodkina
Domino by Claire Masurel
The Doorbell Rang by Pat Hutchins
Harold and the Purple Crayon by Crockett Johnson
When I Feel Good About Myself by Cornelia Maude Spelman
Imogene's Antlers by David Small
Itsy Bitsy Spider by Iza Trapani
Jennie's Hat by Ezra Jack Keats
King of the Playground by Phyllis Naylor
The Little Engine that Could by Watty Piper
Mouse Paint by Ellen Stoll Walsh
Mr. Pine's Purple House by Leonard Kessler
Pickle-Chiffon Pie by Jolly Roger Bradfield
Swimmy by Leo Lionni
Where the Wild Things Are by Maurice Sendak

Practice Confidence
● **Challenge children to the edge of their competencies.** Children learn and grow when they have opportunities to practice newly acquired skills as well as when they experience a challenge just beyond the level of their present mastery. Children are motivated and feel more successful when they face and then accomplish slightly difficult tasks or activities.
  ● Match activities to the child's emerging needs and interests.
  ● Challenge the child, but not to the point of frustration. Target experiences to the edge of the child's changing capacities.
  ● Never underestimate a child's abilities.
  ● Work with the child on challenging projects. Offer suggestions for trying new ways to accomplish tasks. Refrain from helping too much.

- **Keep physical space cozy.** Children feel large in relation to their environment. Maria Montessori demonstrated her knowledge of this fact when she designed child-size furniture.
  - Create small play areas.
  - Create private spaces where the child can be alone. For example, you might create a reading "tent" or an oversized cardboard "get away" box.

- **Avoid perfectionism.** Insisting that blocks line up perfectly or only accepting art that is aesthetically pleasing leads children to believe that anything less than perfect is unacceptable. Perfectionism can lead children to be afraid to try new things, become over-sensitive to criticism, and procrastinate.
  - Teach the child to set high, yet attainable, standards. This is the hallmark of a healthy striver.
  - Accept the child's efforts and celebrate her determination and persistence instead of focusing on a perfect outcome.
  - Celebrate mistakes as opportunities for learning. Thomas Edison said, "If I find 10,000 ways something won't work, I haven't failed. I am not discouraged, because every wrong attempt discarded is another step forward." Everyone makes mistakes. Learning from our mistakes is what matters.
  - Model the acceptance of criticism. Help the child view it as a means for learning and growing instead of something to avoid.
  - Teach the child to enjoy the process of creating. This is especially easy when she is drawing or painting, where the opportunity for creativity is high.
  - Teach the child to self-assess with fairness. Help her understand that what she thinks of her efforts provides motivation to move forward. Outside evaluations can be helpful, but they are certainly less accurate than one's self-evaluation. Help the child understand that outside evaluations do not define who she is.
  - Ask questions that help the child self-assess. For example, say, "Building that fort took determination. How does that make you feel?" or "Why do you think you're having trouble getting your tower to stay up?"
  - Perfectionism is often fueled by rigid thinking. Often, perfectionists won't let go of an idea, even when they know they should. Animals exhibit the same rigid thinking that often appears with human perfectionist behaviors. "The South Indian Monkey Trap Fable" on page 30 shows what can happen to victims of rigid thinking—whether they happen to be humans or monkeys!

> "Whether you think that you can or you can't, you're usually right."
> —Henry Ford

The South Indian Monkey Trap Fable

Some villagers in India developed a trap to catch small monkeys. They hollowed out a coconut, made a hole in it that was just big enough for a monkey's hand to fit through, and chained it to a stake. Then, the villagers placed some rice inside the coconut.

Tempted by the rice, monkeys reached in and became trapped because the hole in the coconut was too small for them to remove their rice-filled fists. The monkeys did not understand that if they let go of what they wanted—the rice—they could be free. If they rigidly held on to the rice, they would be captured. Most of the time, the trap worked and the villagers captured the monkeys.

- **Encourage persistence.**
  - A child needs time to focus on the activity she is engaged in without interruption. Instead of trying to help her finish what she is doing so you can move on, allow ample time for the child to focus on the task at hand and plenty of notice before moving on to something else.
  - Think of an activity that you can teach the child in which she will visibly improve over time. For example, you might start doing jumping jacks every day. At the beginning of the month, write down how many jumping jacks she can do before tiring. Each week, encourage her to beat her "personal best." Use this activity as an example of how you can improve with practice and persistence.

- **Be fully present.**
  - Listen carefully. This is easier said than done. In today's busy world, it is easy to give superficial attention to a child's questions and comments. Instead, really take time to listen and respond constructively and with interest. This helps the child feel that her work and her comments and questions are valid and respected. When you are fully present with the child, she feels that she is the most important person in the world.

- When you get frustrated, take a moment to calm down before responding or acting. Being fully present for the child requires your full attention, and frustration is a distraction.
- Teach the child how to be "fully present." Help her practice how to listen attentively and respond appropriately.

- **Practice problem solving.** When children solve problems, they feel confident. This confidence motivates children to tackle new and challenging situations, which in turn leads to greater learning.
  - Encourage hands-on investigations. Hands-on experimentation allows the child to use trial and error as she learns about the things in hers world.
    - Provide interesting items to explore, such as rocks, leaves, kitchen gadgets, old clocks, boat parts, pulleys, and so on.
    - Rotate toys and other items to keep them fresh and thought-provoking. Put some toys and materials away and take them out when children need a fresh look or a new challenge. Begin with activities that encourage the child to count to three and gradually add activities that encourage counting to four, five, six, and so on. Build an understanding from simple to more complex. For example, before you expect the child to classify materials (sort by likenesses), provide activities that teach the math vocabulary required for classifying, such as descriptive words like "round," "square," "tall," "short," "thick," "thin," "red," "blue," and directional words like "up," "down," "in," "out," and "inside." With this preparation, the child has the tools she needs to be successful when asked to place the red items inside the square box.
    - Provide unique items for water play. Offer funnels and containers some of the time, and basters and sponges at other times. Invite the child to use all kinds of interesting items for water play, including hand beaters, whisks, measuring spoons, tubing, corks, and pumps.

- **Foster creative and critical thinking skills** by encouraging children to use items in new ways.
  - Make megaphones from empty paper towel tubes. Use cylindrical building blocks, hair rollers, or curlers as microphones.

- Use a variety of items as paintbrushes, such as feathers, squeegees, twigs, corn husks, feather dusters, or spatulas. How do these different paintbrushes change the outcome of the painting?
- Make funnels. Demonstrate how you can make a funnel by rolling a sheet of paper diagonally.
- Explore ways to move pieces of Styrofoam. Invite the child to think of ways to move a Styrofoam chip from one end of a table to the other without using her hands.
- What can you do with a paper bag? Give the child a small paper bag. Ask her what she can do with the bag, other than use it to carry something.

- **Encourage children's suggestions and solutions.** Listen carefully to the children's ideas. Offer help when they become frustrated, but don't solve their problems. Learning to control frustration develops emotional security, which is the ability to control emotions and to maintain an emotional balance. When children know they can find a solution to a problem, they are less likely to become overly worried about it. Each time they solve a problem, they become more certain that they will be able to solve future problems. This cycle leads them to become more patient and less frustrated.
  - Discuss the steps in problem solving. Use the following questions to help the child focus on the problem and the solution.
    Step 1: What's my problem?
    Step 2: What are my choices to solve it?
    Step 3: What looks like the best way?
    Step 4: What can I do myself to solve it?
            What help do I need from someone else?
    Step 5: Try my solution.
    Step 6: Decide if it worked or if I should do something differently.
  - Challenge the child to solve problems:
    Problem: The wagon is stuck in the mud.
    Question: How can we get it out?

    Problem: Our ball is in a big puddle of water.
    Question: How can we get it out?

    Problem: I need to move across the floor but I cannot use my feet.
    Question: How can I get across the floor?

    Problem: The papers keep blowing off the table.
    Question: How can we keep them on the table?

- Encourage the child to think of new ways to use materials. For example, ask the child to think of ways she might use scarves to create a costume.
- Encourage the child to help others. For example, if the child is a more advanced "puzzler worker," suggest that she help her friend who is less advanced at working with puzzles.

- **Ask open-ended questions.**
  - "What can you do with a clothespin (bottle cap, jar lid, feather, paper clip)?"
  - "How many ways can you use a ball (crayon, block, wagon)?"
  - "If we need to move the water in this bucket to a new location without moving the bucket, how can we move the water?"

- **Encourage children to talk out loud when problem solving.** Often, a young child will talk herself through a series of actions to find the solution to a problem. As the child matures, this "talking out loud" will become an internal monologue.

- **Use encouragement, not praise.** Praise is external. External rewards inhibit internal motivation. Encouragement offers children an opportunity to build internal satisfaction and joy.
  - Eliminate the use of stickers and privilege rewards. Link actions to enjoyment and satisfaction instead of a tangible reward. Examples:
    - Look at you! You finished the puzzle. That took determination."
    - "You did it! You came down the slide feet first and landed right in my arms."
  - Use encouragement especially when the child makes a poor choice. Examples:
    - "I'm sure you can find a better way next time."
    - "What could you say to Madison next time to get her to share her toy?"
  - Be honest and sincere with compliments. Examples:
    - "You used blue. That's my favorite color."
    - "That tower is as tall as you are, Audrey! Is it the tallest tower you have built?"
  - Encourage the child to critique themselves. Give her opportunities to evaluate her own accomplishments. Rather than stating that you think she has done a good job, ask her what she thinks of her work. Examples:

> "You gain strength, courage, and confidence by every experience in which you really stop to look fear in the face."
>
> —Eleanor Roosevelt

- "How did you get the leaves to stay on your paper?"
- "What gave you the idea to use the bowl as a hat?"

- Avoid comparisons. Comparing one child to another creates resentment. The child who serves as your model is left to feel frozen in the role of "good" child. The other child may resent the "good" child for getting your attention.
- Focus on process instead of product. Discuss the colors the child uses in her artwork, the determination she applies to learning a new task, or the courage she exhibits when trying to climb up another rung on the slide ladder. Encouragement during the process creates a joyful experience and reminds the child that creating and doing can be as much fun as finishing.
- Notice and describe behavior. Examples:
  - "You worked hard to finish your building."
  - "You found several ways to arrange the buttons."

- **Encourage independence.** Respond to the child's needs in a consistent, predictable manner as you nudge her to find her own answers. When she asks you a question, ask her, "What do you think?"

- **Break tasks into small parts.** Nudge a reluctant child to complete a task by breaking tasks into smaller parts. For example, maybe help the child practice arranging items by likenesses and differences before you ask her to use the items to create a pattern.

Acknowledge Confidence

- **Help children acknowledge their acts that demonstrate confidence.** When the child directs the problem solving that helps get a block to stay on top of the tower that she built, acknowledge her persistence.

- **Celebrate small steps along the way to success.** Sometimes the child needs to know she is almost there or at least is on the right path.

- **Acknowledge successes** by allowing the child time to talk about her achievements.

● **Participate in brainstorming and problem-solving activities.** Select random items and brainstorm new uses. For example, how might we use a bottle cap for something other than capping a bottle? What can we use a straw for other than drinking? Challenge the child to think of things she can use as accessories as she builds with blocks. What can we use for a bed? Challenge her to think of things to use as pretend food in her play. Can yarn be used for pretend spaghetti?

> "The greatest barrier to success is the fear of failure."
> —*Sven Goran Eriksson*

Reflect on Confidence

● **Ask children questions that will help them think about confidence.**

- How do you feel when you are able to solve a problem?
- What do you do when something seems too difficult?
- What is confidence? How do you feel when you are confident?
- How do you gain confidence?
- What are some examples of confidence?

Curiosity

2

WHAT IS CURIOSITY?

An intense desire to know and to understand; disposition to inquire, investigate, or seek after knowledge; desire to gratify the mind with new information or objects of interest; inquisitiveness. (Adapted from Webster's II New College Dictionary)

Curious children are alert to their senses and keenly aware of their environment. They notice little things like an ant carrying a morsel of food or a new poster on the wall. Curious children ask "why" often and when they get the answer they will often have another question. They are able to sustain interest with or without an adult close by.

A Child Shows Curiosity When...	A Curious Child Understands These Words...	
● She demonstrates interest in the environment and in people.	cause and effect	new
● He explores new materials.	desire	novel
● She asks questions.	discovery	novelty
● He identifies problems and seeks solutions.	experiment	pleasure
● She exhibits persistence and determination.	explore	predict
	fear	question
	imagination	safety
	inquire	seek
	interest	senses
	investigate	wonder
	learn	world
	mastery	

WHY CURIOSITY MATTERS

Curiosity drives intellect. We are born curious, and we immediately begin to use our senses to explore the world around us. Without curiosity, a baby would never reach for a rattle.

Young children are naturally curious. To a child, the world is full of infinite possibilities. Children believe pigs talk, monsters can fit under their beds, and wolves are able to knock down a house with a simple huff and puff. Children's ideas are without limits, judgments, and bias. They enjoy coloring trees purple and the sun green. They are constantly asking who, what, when, where, and why.

Some people remain insatiably curious throughout their lives. Others lose their drive to know, possibly because of societal pressure to perform well on tests and conform to social norms. Without curiosity, learners become passive and compliant. They are more eager to be "right" and to please authority than they are to explore, question, and experiment. They lose their sense of wonder when they cease to exercise it.

Curiosity encourages exploration, questions, experimentation, and a sense of wonder. It solves problems, clarifies values, and strengthens relationships. The more we know, the more tools we have to understand our world and communicate with others.

Bruce Perry (2001) says curiosity drives exploration and results in discovery, which leads to pleasure and repetition. Repetition leads to mastery and confidence, which in turn leads to continued exploration. This cycle is the foundation of learning. Curiosity is the catalyst.

Curiosity	results in	Exploration
Exploration	results in	Discovery
Discovery	results in	Pleasure
Pleasure	results in	Repetition
Repetition	results in	Mastery
Mastery	results in	New Skills
New Skills	results in	Confidence
Confidence	results in	Self-Esteem
Self-Esteem	results in	Sense of Security
Security	results in	More Exploration

Perry, Bruce (2001) "Curiosity: The Fuel of Development." Early Childhood Today, NY, Scholastic.

WHAT THE RESEARCH SAYS

● The brain is designed to reward our curiosity. Novelty produces opiates, which create a sense of well-being and lift our mood.

● Curiosity is innate.

(ScienceDaily, 2006; Jowles, 2004)

WHAT YOU CAN DO TO BOOST A CHILD'S CURIOSITY SKILLS

Model Curiosity

● **Use "I wonder" statements.** Say things like, "I wonder what would happen if we put these two things together." "I wonder why blocks don't bounce." Encourage the child to answer your "I wonder" statements. If he can't come up with a probable answer, then help him by asking questions that might lead him to an answer. For example, in trying to help him answer the "I wonder" statement about blocks, ask, "Can you think of some things that bounce?"

● **When you find something unusual, talk about it.** Encourage the child to say what he finds unusual about the item.

● **When things make you curious, say so aloud,** "I'm curious about why it is raining today." "I'm curious why that beanbag always lands with the yellow side up."

● **Ask "what if" questions.** What if the only colors we had were blue and green? What color would milk be? Would it taste different? What if elephants could fly? Where would they roost? What if children were in charge of adults? Read *Nonsense* by Sally Kahler Phillips. Discuss the nonsense statements in the book.

Talk About Curiosity

● **Define curiosity.** Explain to the child that curiosity is a desire to know more. Ask the child what he is curious about.

● **Use the quote, "Curiosity killed the cat" as a stimulus for discussion.** Encourage the child to describe the behavior of the cats. Why would someone say that curiosity killed the cat? Do you think curiosity really killed the cat? Is curiosity a good thing? Why? Does curiosity ever get you in trouble? Why? How can our curiosity help us learn?

● **Create an "Investigator's Corner" or an "Items of Interest" box.** Place unusual items in a specific place. For example, a special seashell, snake skin, locust skeletons, rocks and stones, old pairs of sunglasses, music boxes, and magnets. Help the child learn to pose questions about these items.

● **Read books about curiosity** and discuss the role curiosity plays in the story. For example, in *Who Is the Beast?* by Keith Baker, the tiger is curious about why all the animals run from him. What does he find out? Did his curiosity lead to him to find out something good? Here are some other books with themes related to curiosity.

Curious George by H. A. Rey
Edward the Emu by Sheena Knowles
Henny Penny (traditional, many versions available)
How Come? by Kathy Wollard
If You Give a Mouse a Cookie by Laura Joffe Numeroff
In the Forest by Gallimara-Jeunesse
The Monster at the End of this Book by Jon Stone and Michael Smollin
Nonsense by Sally Kahler Phillips
The Nose Knows by Ellen Weiss
The Rainbow Mystery by Jennifer Dussling
What's that Sound? by Mary Lawrence
Who Is the Beast by Keith Baker
Why? by Catherine Ripley

> "A sense of curiosity is nature's original school of education."
> —Smiley Blanton

Practice Curiosity

● **Allow children to explore and "fall in love" with their environment.**
  ● Keep the environment safe for exploration.
  ● Stimulate children's senses. Young children's senses are in a heightened state of awareness. This provides a great opportunity to help the child explore and

expand his understanding of the world through a variety of sensory activities/experiences. Discuss how things feel, smell, taste (if possible), sound, and look. Focus on the colors, shapes, textures, tastes, and sounds of things in the environment.

- Provide materials, such as gears, pulleys, chains, seeds, rocks, leaves, feathers, hair, bark from trees and bushes, and other items that are new to the child. When your toaster breaks, don't throw it away. Instead, cut off the plug and let the child take it apart.

> "Curiosity is the very basis of education and if you tell me that curiosity killed the cat, I say only the cat died nobly."
> —*Arnold Edinborough*

- Take frequent walks outdoors. Point out unusual plant and animal life. Point out interesting things in the sky (clouds, birds, dust, and debris in a wind gust). Watch a butterfly. Listen to the wind as it blows through the trees.

- Comment and expand upon the child's fascinations. For example, if the child finds a ladybug outside, use it as a springboard for further information. Count its spots. Look at it with a magnifying glass. Let it crawl on his arm. It will be more meaningful to him when he discovers it.

- Encourage the child to use his senses outdoors. Take time to listen to wind chimes. Watch raindrops drip down windowpanes. Point out differences in sand and mud.

- Engage the child in simple, hands-on experiments, such as sink-and-float games, planting and caring for seeds, and classifying objects that stick or do not stick to a magnet.

- Provide investigation tools, such as magnifying glasses, tuning forks, magnets, funnels, scales, prisms, tweezers, measuring tape, balancing scales, tongs, and bug catchers.

- Stimulate the child's imagination. For example:
  - Have the child pretend he is a raindrop. What does a raindrop feel like during a thunderstorm? How does it feel during a sprinkle?
  - When the child is not looking, turn over a table. Ask the child how he thinks it happened.
  - When the child is not looking or is out of the room, sprinkle glitter on a table. Ask the child where he thinks the glitter came from.
  - Build a bed for a giant with blocks.
  - Ask the child to describe what types of equipment he might need if he were suddenly asked to take care of a dinosaur.

- Listen to the child's description of his dreams. Show interest. Ask questions. Sometimes just listening with interest is all that is necessary, but if activities help to nurture the child's dreams then follow up with those activities. If the child tells you he wants to work in a zoo when he grows up, take a trip to the zoo. Help him collect photos of animals and categorize them in a binder. Read books about people who work with animals. If the child talks about wanting to see the North Pole, find ways to help him gain more information about the North Pole. Show him where the North Pole is on a globe. Discuss the weather at the North Pole.

- Encourage the child to believe in magic—princesses that feel pebbles under 42 mattresses, giants with gooses that lay golden eggs, animals that talk, puppets with noses that grow when they tell a lie, and fairies that make wishes come true. The child will learn soon enough what is real and what is make-believe. Make sure he knows that it is okay to enjoy the pleasures of "make-believe."
- Tell a story or read a book and then ask, "How would the story be different if _____?"
- Turn questions into a quest. If the child asks you a question, use it as a door to discovery. If you don't know the answer, research it.
- Ask questions that stimulate thinking:
  - How do you know _____?
  - Why do you say that?
  - What do you mean by _____?
  - What would happen if _____?
  - What would you like to know?
- Accept the non-traditional. It is all right if the child colors the sky pink and the leaves on the tree blue. It's fine if he chooses to wear his jacket backwards.
- Show the child interesting or unusual things, such as your high-school yearbook, your baby book, a blanket you knitted, or a birdhouse you painted.
- Plant milkweed and see how many butterflies it attracts. Encourage the child to learn more about butterflies and what attracts them.
- Make Goop and Gak (see page 109). Compare the two substances.
- Develop a secret code. Teach the child how to use it. For example, use a hand signal to communicate an idea, such as pulling on your ear when you see the child doing something nice. Use other special signals to say "hello" or "goodbye."
- Give the child sheets of colored cellophane for him to make color shadows wherever possible both indoors and outdoors.
- Create a "mystery box." Decorate a box with question marks. Place interesting things inside the box. Give the child clues to help him determine what the mystery item might be.
- Set up treasure hunts using rebus picture clues.

- **Redefine failure.** Failure leads to frustration and unattended frustration ends with giving up.
  - Explain that failing is a part of learning. When we get it wrong, we are one step closer to getting it right.
  - Discuss failures you have encountered. Did they eventually end in success?
  - Point out how the Itsy Bitsy Spider's refusal to give up her goal of climbing the waterspout shows determination. Define determination and persistence. (Determination can be defined as an intention to do something, and persistence as continuing to work toward a goal no matter the obstacles.) Ask the child to describe things he has struggled to learn, such as how to catch a ball or pour a glass of juice without spilling it.

- **Reinforce cause-and-effect relationships.**
  - Cause and effect are at the core of curiosity and the base of cognitive development. Cause-and-effect relationships play a part in problem solving when a solution to a problem is being selected and tested.
  - Cause-and-effect relationships are everywhere. If you tease a dog, it will growl. If you practice riding a bike, you will get better. If you go to bed late, you will be tired the next day. If you kick a ball, it will roll. However, when these things happen, do not assume that the child sees the relationship. For example, if the blocks tumble down, ask the child what happened. If he can't explain the relationship between the way the blocks were stacked and the blocks falling, explain the relationship.
  - With an older child, point out words that signal a cause-and-effect relationship, such as "because," "so," "therefore," "if...then," "consequently," "as a result of," "due to," "nevertheless," and "thus." Encourage the child to practice putting sentences together that express a cause-and-effect relationship. For example, "The ball moved because I kicked it," or "The blocks fell because they were stacked unevenly."
  - Read books that have a cause-and-effect storylines, such as *Rosie's Walk* by Pat Hutchins, *If You Give a Mouse a Cookie,* or *If You Give a Moose a Muffin* by Laura Joffe Numeroff. Discuss the-cause-and effect relationships in the books.

> "Curiosity is the wick in the candle of learning."
>
> —William Arthur Ward

● **Read chapter books.** Between chapters, ask challenging questions for the child to think about. "What do you think will happen to the lemon pudding that Julian's father made?" (from *The Stories That Julian Tells* by Ann Cameron). Waiting to hear the end of the story builds suspense and curiosity. Here are a few chapter books that work well with preschoolers:

Frog and Toad Together by Arnold Lobel
Little Bear by Else Holmelund Minarik
Tales of Oliver Pig by Jean Van Leeuwen
The Stories That Julian Tells by Ann Cameron

Acknowledge Curiosity

● **Help children learn more about their interests.** When the child shows interest in something, help him discover more by connecting his interest to a book or activity. For example, if the child is interested in shadows, extend his learning by letting him create indoor shadows by stepping between a light source (flashlight or canister uplight) and a wall, by reading him the poem, "My Shadow" by Robert Lewis Stevenson, by providing objects to be matched to their shadows, and so on.

● **Be interested in what children find interesting.** Talk with the child about what he is curious about and interested in. This will reinforce his interests. Sharing his interests also shows that you value his thinking.

Reflect on Curiosity

● **Ask children questions that encourage them to think about curiosity.**
  ● What sparks your curiosity? What interests you?
  ● What do you do when you see something you have not seen before?
  ● What is the most interesting thing you have seen lately?
  ● What is the most interesting thing you have done lately?
  ● How do you feel when you learn or discover something you didn't know? Do you share the finding with someone? Who?

Intentionality

3

WHAT IS INTENTIONALITY?

Acting with intention on a course of action or an aim that one intends to follow; a plan to achieve; setting a goal. (Adapted from Webster's II New College Dictionary)

Children who are intentional think before acting. They consider their choices before choosing. They make a plan before they start a project. Intentional children are competent and effective.

A Child Shows Intentionality When...	An Intentional Child Understands These Words...	
• She makes thoughtful choices.	actions	goal
• He considers alternatives.	choices	intent
• She understands the difference in thoughts and actions.	commitment	persistent
	consider	purpose
• He finishes work.	do	reflection
• She demonstrates persistence and determination.	drive	satisfaction
	effectiveness	think
• He acts with confidence.	focus	

Why Intentionality Matters

When an infant moves a blanket to find a toy underneath, she has a goal and she accomplishes it with an action. Her actions are based on cause and effect. "I want the toy. I move the blanket. I get the toy." This is intention.

It is important during the early years to help children set appropriate goals and teach them strategies (tools) that help them achieve their goals. Often children know what they want; they just don't know how to get it. They know what they want to do; they just don't know how to accomplish it.

Children learn by doing. If we want children to be able to set and achieve goals successfully then we need to provide experiences that allow them to practice making intentional choices. Ultimately, we want children to combine their self-confidence with their intentionality. Individuals who are secure in their choices are more likely to achieve their goals because they don't waiver; they move forward with confidence. Individuals who are secure in their choices are more likely to inspire the confidence of others and, therefore, are more likely to ask others for help. These individuals are more likely to move successfully through the ups and downs of life.

Helping children develop intentionality requires helping them learn to ask themselves *what, why,* and *how* questions. *Why* do you want to paint today? *What* would you like to do outdoors? *Why* do you feel sad? *How* can you build a really big house with blocks? The answers may provide important information and help children clarify their intentions.

When we act without intentionality we are acting as a creature of habit or a creature of event and circumstance. For example, many children choose to play with a toy based on comfort and familiarity or based on what a friend is playing (a choice that follows someone else's intentionality). When intentionality and purpose guide decision making, decisions move us toward our personal goals.

WHAT THE RESEARCH SAYS
- Two types of neurons are activated in the brain when humans interact with others. Mirror cells apparently play a role in both the setting and the achieving of our goals. Mirror cells are active both when we act on our own intentions and when we attempt to determine the intentions of others by observing their behaviors. Spindle cells, which are only present in humans, enable us to make a snap judgment about another person's intentions .
- Preschool children can not make thoughtful decisions when they are given more than three options to choose from .

(Bower, 2005; Jensen, 2005; Kines, 1998)

WHAT YOU CAN DO TO BOOST A CHILD'S INTENTIONALITY SKILLS

Model Intentionality

- **Talk about your plans.** Talk with the child about how you make decisions about the day. Explain that you plan things for her to do that will help her learn, that you are intentional.

- **Point out examples of intentional thinking.** When things occur that are examples of intentional thinking, point them out. For example, point out why you select certain foods for lunch. Explain that you chose the foods for specific reasons—nutrition, things the child likes, foods that are easy to serve, and so on.

- **Let children know when you are thinking about something.** When the child asks you questions that require some thought, for example, "Can we stay outside a little longer?" or "May I have an extra cookie?" say, "Let me think about that for a minute." When you give your answer, explain the reason or reasons for your answer.

Talk About Intentionality

- **Discuss the importance of thinking about what we want to do and what we want to accomplish.** Point out intentional decisions that families make, such as where they want to live or what car they wish to buy. Point out opportunities the child has for making decisions. Who will she play with? What color will she use for the monster she is painting? Who will she invite to her birthday party? Ask the child, "What happens when we don't think before we act?"

> "The road is long from the intention to the completion."
>
> —Moliere, Le Tartuffe

- **Read stories that feature characters who make intentional choices.** For example, in the story *Flower Garden* by Eve Bunting, a little girl and her father carefully plan a colorful birthday surprise for her mom. They buy soil, a pot, and flowers and make a flower garden for the mom's birthday present. After reading the story, ask the child questions that highlight how the characters made choices. "How did the girl and her father decide to make a flower garden?" "Why?" "How did they make sure they had everything they needed?" "What would have happened if they had not been thoughtful and careful to get everything they needed?"

> "Right intention is to the actions of a man what the soul is to the body, or the root to the tree."
>
> —Jeremy Taylor

Here are some books that relate to intentionality:

A Chair for My Mother by Vera Williams
Amazing Grace by Mary Hoffman
Dream Carver by Diana Cohn
Itsy Bitsy Spider by Iza Trapani
The Little Engine that Could by Watty Piper
The Little Painter of Sabana Grande by Patricia Markum
The Little Red Hen (traditional, many versions available)
Something Special for Me by Vera Williams

Practice Intentionality: Intentionality-Building Strategies and Activities

- **Offer choices.** This allows children to practice making thoughtful choices.
  - Offer the child a limited number of options so that she can easily assess the pros and cons of each possibility. This optimizes her ability to make thoughtful choices (Morrison, 1997).
  - Read books and then use the choices that characters in books make as a springboard for a discussion about intentionality.
    - "The little red hen chose not to share her bread with her friends because they didn't help her bake the bread. Do you think this was a good decision? Why?"
    - "In the story of 'The Three Little Pigs,' the first and second pigs chose to build their houses from materials that would allow them to finish building quickly so they could play. Was this a good decision? Why? Which material would you have chosen? Why?"
    - "In the story of 'The Three Billy Goats Gruff,' the small- and medium-size goats told the troll to wait for their brother. Was this a good decision? Why?"

- **Discuss the difference between doing what we want to do and doing the right thing.**
  - Provide scenarios that demonstrate the difference between "want" and "right" and talk about them.
    - "I accidentally took Christopher's car home in my pocket. I like it and I want to keep it. What is the right thing to do?"
    - "Corrine snatched the book I was reading from my hand. I want to snatch it back. What is the right thing to do?"
    - "I can have one cookie. I am hungry. I want two cookies. What is the right thing to do?"

- "It's time to clean up and I am not finished with my picture. What is the right thing to do?"
- "I told Riley I want to play with the red shoes she is wearing. She said, 'No way!' What is the right thing to do?"

- Discuss the difference between "need" and "want." Provide a list of items or photos of items that the child may need and some she may want. Show the photos and have the child classify each item as a need or a want.

- **Allow time for focusing and reflecting.** This provides time for children to really think about what they are learning from beginning to end.
  - Make sure the child is focused before you provide information. Neurological research states that in order for information to make its way into the brain the learner must be focused.
    - Ask questions or make statements that get the child's attention. Say, "Tell me what you know about (name a topic)." "What would you like to learn about (a topic)?"
    - Show photos or concrete objects related to the information.
    - Use a related song, fingerplay, chant, or poem to help direct the child's attention.
  - Give children time to reflect on information they have learned.
    - Ask thinking questions. For example,
      - "Giraffes have long necks and long legs. What might be good about having long legs and a long neck? What other animals have long necks and long legs?"
      - "Today we learned some things about giraffes and elephants. How are giraffes different from elephants?"
      - "Which character in the story would you prefer to be? Why?"
  - Make sure your questions help the child make sense and meaning of the new information she is learning by offering her a structure for comparison. For example, ask, "How is this new information like something else we have learned?" or "How will we use this information?" If the information was about zoo animals, ask, "How are zoo animals like farm animals?" "How are they different?" "Why is it important to know which animals are found on farms and which animals are found at the zoo?"

- **Encourage persistence and commitment.**
  - Insist that the child finish what she started. If a child begins working on a puzzle, she must finish it before starting something else. When the child must finish what she starts, she will learn to think more intently before she starts a project rather than starting a project simply because she wants to. She might find that she enjoys the project more than she anticipated.
  - Create a "Tomorrow Box" where the child can store unfinished artwork to finish later.
  - Offer projects that develop over time, such as planning and planting a garden and caring for it or cooking a recipe that takes a few steps or hours to complete (baking bread or making gelatin).
  - Help the child celebrate small successes on the way to a complete success. For example, if a child is trying to write her name she might first celebrate the joy of finding each letter she will use on an alphabet chart or in the box of plastic letters.
  - Teach the child how to sing "Itsy Bitsy Spider," which is a story of persistence and determination. The spider didn't quit; she dried off and started again. Ask the child to think of something she has accomplished that took several tries.
  - Help the child if she is struggling to complete a project. Model and encourage new ways to think about how to finish the work.
  - Discuss marathon races. Help the child understand that a marathon is a long distance (26.2 miles). Perhaps you can best illustrate the distance by telling the child how many laps it would be around the playground. "Run" a marathon. Mark a spot that is a quarter-mile away (or closer for younger children). Run or walk that distance every day. Keep track of the mileage every day by moving a paper doll along a line on the wall that represents the distance of 26.2 miles. When you finish the marathon distance, have a celebration. Remind the child that it took many small steps to run the full distance and that there are some projects that require a little bit of work at a time.

- **Encourage the development of internal satisfaction.**
  - Challenge the child. Each of us is more stimulated when working toward meaningful goals. Internal satisfaction should be a guide for making choices.
    - Encourage the child to set goals. For example, ask, "Abby, how many beanbags do you think you can get into the box if you are standing behind this line?"
    - Help the child set goals that are achievable but require effort. Balance abilities and limitations. For example, if a child is proficient at creating vertical patterns suggest that she try circular patterns.

SEVEN SKILLS FOR SCHOOL SUCCESS

- Each day, ask the child to set goals for what she wants to accomplish. She can draw what she intends to do or she can dictate a sentence or two about what she wants to do. At the end of the day, review her plan to see if she met her goal.

- **Stimulate children's curiosity.** Curiosity sparks an internal quest that encourages the making of thoughtful choices. See pages 37–44 for other ideas that foster curiosity.
  - Ask "what if" questions.
    - "What if birds had four legs instead of two?"
    - "What if there was no such thing as the color blue? What color would the sky be? How would that change the way the clouds look?"
    - "What if people could fly?"
    - "What if we mix these things together? Salt and water? Blue playdough and yellow playdough? Glue and starch?"
  - Present things that cause the child to rethink what she knows. For example, when she becomes skilled at stringing beads, change the direction from down to up. Attach one end of the string to a table with masking tape. The child sits on the floor and strings beads up the string.
  - After reading a story, ask, "How would the story be different if _____? For example, how would the story of the 'Gingerbread Man' be different if he hadn't run away? What if he hadn't allowed the fox to persuade him to hop on his nose?"

- **Share control.** The desire for control is a natural human tendency. All humans need to feel as if they have control over themselves and their lives.
  - Allow the child to have choices as often as possible. Choices motivate learners. Choices help the child feel that she is an active participant in learning. Help her be intentional in making choices by talking with her about her options. Make sure she has the information she needs to make a wise choice.
  - Connect current learning to future use. This makes learning meaningful and relevant. "If you learn to count, think of all the things you can keep track of—the number of days until your birthday, the number of balls we are taking to the playground, how many candles are on Don's birthday cake, and so much more!"

"Ultimately, human intentionality is the most powerful evolutionary force on this planet."
—George Leonard

- **Encourage cooperation.** Cooperation is shared intentionality. Helping others and receiving help from others feels good. See page 77 for ideas for promoting cooperation.
  - Play cooperative games (pages 92–94).
  - Ask the child to help you when appropriate. "I am trying to put the books back on the bookshelf. Will you help?"

Acknowledge Intentionality

- **Acknowledge children's successes.** For example, "Today you started the swing going all by yourself. All the times you tried to start the swing really paid off."

- **Sustained effort (persistence) deserves recognition.** "Alice, you are determined to get that ball in the net. You are getting closer with every toss."

Reflect on Intentionality

- **Ask children questions that encourage them to think about intentionality.**
  - How do you choose which toy you want to play with?
  - Why is it important to think before you act?
  - How do you decide what you want to do when you go outside?
  - When you get dressed in the morning, what do you think about before you select your clothes?

SEVEN SKILLS FOR SCHOOL SUCCESS

Self-Control

4

WHAT IS SELF-CONTROL?

The ability to control one's emotions, desires, or actions by one's own will; staying calm and productive during high-stress situations. (Adapted from Webster's II New College Dictionary)

Children with self-control understand their emotional reactions and are able to calm their emotions before acting. They are able to control their impulses. They are able to listen attentively. They can wait patiently. Children with self-control are able to accept and stay within boundaries.

A Child Shows Self-Control When...	A Child With Self-Control Understands These Words...	
● She controls impulses.	action	patience
● He delays gratification.	behavior	problem solve
● She understands the difference between thoughts and actions.	conflicts	resolve
	consequences	responsibility
● He expresses emotions appropriately.	control	rules
	emotions	safe
● She follows rules.	fair	wait
● He respects the boundaries of others.	feelings	

WHY SELF-CONTROL MATTERS

Children who can control their own actions have self-control. Having self-control means knowing right from wrong. Self-control wires in the brain as children experience making choices and practice accepting limits. Children who rely on others (friends, parents, and teachers) to make choices for them do not develop self-control because they do not get the opportunity to practice. These children may follow the "poor" choices of others.

Self-control develops as children learn that there are limits to their behavior. They learn that those limits (boundaries) cannot be altered by any amount of screaming, kicking, crying, stomping, begging, or bargaining. Research shows that self-control begins to wire in the brain as early as 16 months (Ramey & Ramey, 1999). This can be problematic because it happens at a time when some parents may have difficulty setting and maintaining boundaries, especially with toddlers. Whether in the middle of a crowded mall, at a dinner with extended family, or even at home, temper tantrums are frustrating. Parents sometimes give in to save embarrassment and other times just to stop the noise.

Sometimes, adults make the mistake of believing that toddlers are too young to understand that they must accept limits. Toddlers actually learn quickly that boundaries are non-negotiable when adults consistently hold the line. Allowing children to have their way because of their tantrums wires the brain for lack of impulse control. That wiring will have to be rewired if the child is to ever learn self-control.

When children learn to exercise self-control, they make better choices and they are more likely to respond properly to stressful situations. For example, if you tell a child that he can have a cookie after he finishes his lunch, a child who exercises self-control will accept that limit. Children with self-control are able to postpone gratification, and they are able to control their impulses to beg and plead. They understand that if they make a fuss or beg and plead, their actions may cause you to take away the cookie entirely. If you make the same statement to a child who is not able to exercise self-control, he might cry, throw a tantrum, or plead in hopes that you will give in and allow him to have the cookie on his timetable instead of the timetable you have set as a boundary.

According to some researchers (Shoda et al, 1960), self-control is the most important skill a child must exhibit to be successful in school. Consider the following "Marshmallow Experiment."

The Marshmallow Experiment is a famous research study conducted by Walter Mischel at Stanford University in the 1960s. The purpose of this study was to determine the long-term benefit of a four-year-old's ability to delay gratification and control his impulses. A classroom of four-year-olds was told that they each could have one marshmallow right away, but if they could wait for the researcher to run an errand and return, they each could have two marshmallows. The marshmallows were left on the table while the researcher ran his errand. Cameras were mounted all around the room. The children who took a marshmallow while the researcher was gone were moved into group A. The remainder of the children who chose to wait for two marshmallows formed group B.

The researchers found that when they followed the progress of each child into adolescence, the children in group B (children who waited) were more positive, self-motivated, persistent in the face of difficulties, and able to delay gratification in the pursuit of goals (determined by a survey of parents and teachers).

These good habits lead to higher paying jobs, more enduring relationships, and better general health. Children in group B also scored an average of 210 points higher on the SAT.

Children in group A (children who could not wait) were troubled, stubborn, indecisive, mistrustful, and less self-confident. And, they were still unable to delay immediate gratification.

The researchers concluded that distraction and the desire for instant gratification got in the way of good, focused study time. If not corrected, lack of impulse control will continue to trouble these children throughout their lives. This could result in unsuccessful marriages, low job satisfaction, and as a result, low income, bad health, and all-around frustration with life. This study demonstrated just how important self-control is to lifelong learning. (Shoda, Mischel, & Peake, 1990)

WHAT YOU CAN DO TO BOOST A CHILD'S SELF-CONTROL SKILLS

Model Self-Control

● **Maintain control when children are out of control.** This is not always easy to do. Count to 10, take deep breaths, or do whatever it takes to maintain your composure.

● **Share your emotions with children.** Let the child know when you are especially happy about something—your sister's baby has arrived, or you are excited about going on vacation with your family. Let the child know when you are sad. Explain to him how you are handling your sadness if you think it is something he will understand.

● **Describe what you do to stay in control.** For example, when something happens that almost causes you to lose control, say to the child, "I almost raised my voice, but then I realized that is not a good choice. So I counted to 10 and used my words to tell you again that I needed you to pick up the blocks."

Talk About Self-Control

● **When children are out of control, talk with them about ways to handle their emotions.** Demonstrate to the child how to take deep breaths, count to 10, bringing his hands together at his waist, and so on.

● **Read books that have themes related to self-control.** For example, *Don't Feed the Monster on Tuesdays!* by Adolph Moser or *How to Take the Grrrr out of Anger* by Elizabeth Verdick. Here are other books that have themes related to self-control:

Be Brown by Barbara Bottner
Be Polite and Kind by Cheri Meiners
Don't Rant and Rave on Wednesdays! by Adolph Moser
Feelings by Aliki
Feet Are Not for Kicking by Elizabeth Verdick
Hands Are Not for Hitting by Martine Agassi
Harry the Dirty Dog by Gene Zion
Julius, the Baby of the World by Kevin Henkes
Know and Follow Rules by Cheri Meiners
Noisy Nora by Rosemary Wells
Share and Take Turns by Cheri Meiners
Talk and Work It Out by Cheri Meiners
The Way I Feel by Janan Cain
When I Feel Angry by Cornelia Maude Spelman
Where the Wild Things Are by Maurice Sendak
Words Are Not for Hurting by Elizabeth Verdick

Practice Self-Control

● **Ensure that children's physical needs are met.** Look at the environment from the eyes of the child. Are there things in the classroom that may be frightening, such as a bully, an overly loud caregiver, or visitors that may be perceived as strangers? Children who feel unsafe are anxious. They express their fears in a variety of ways. For example, through constant thoughts about monsters or other scary things; through restless, overly active behavior; or through aggressive behavior.

  ● Think carefully about the information in curriculum topics. Choose vocabulary that is not frightening. For example, when talking about the role of a firefighter, police officer, or doctor, carefully choose your words. For example, instead of saying firefighters look scary in their clothing, say they look odd; or instead of saying a police officer shoots people, say an officer keeps us safe.

- Make sure a non-English-speaking child has a way to communicate his needs. Bring in a parent volunteer. Teach the child sign language. Provide plenty of visuals.
- Avoid bringing things into your classroom or home that may frighten the child, such as costume characters or animals.

- Watch the child for signs of hunger, weariness, and illness. When he is not feeling well or is tired he may be grumpy and out of sorts. This makes self-control more difficult to practice.
- Use safety rituals. Each morning, say, "We take care of each other. You are safe with me always."

- **Teach children stress management.** A child's stress is equal to an adult's stress. The difference is that the child's stress comes in a different package, and he has no idea how to manage it. Here are stress reducers you can teach the child to use.
  - Bring your hands to the center of your body (clasp at waist). This centers the brain. It calms down both hemispheres of the brain and allows thinking to become more focused.
  - Stretch. This loosens tight muscles.
  - Listen to relaxing music. Relaxing music organizes the patterns in the brain. It makes you feel calm and relaxed.
  - Talk to a friend. Sometimes just putting thoughts into words is enough to reduce tension.
  - Take deep breaths. Breathing sends oxygen to the brain, which helps you feel less stressed.
  - Exercise. Physical activity increases endorphins. Higher endorphin levels lower cortisol (stress hormone) levels.
  - Take imaginary trips. Fantasy provides a distraction from reality.

- **Use clear, simple rules. Maintain boundaries.**
  - Fewer rules are better than many rules. Children have difficulty remembering rules if there are too many. Try using a general rule that covers most things. For example, a rule might be, "You can do anything you want as

long as your actions do not hurt yourself or others."

- Let the child help set the rules. If he participates in deciding what the rules should be, he is more likely to remember and follow them.

- As you interpret the rules, make sure you have appropriate expectations. For example, children have short attention spans. The general rule is, one minute per year of age multiplied by three equals a child's fully-developed attention span. Following this rule, a four-year-old will have a 12-minute attention span. Therefore, a four-year-old is not likely to be able to sit and listen for 20 minutes. Design a schedule that reflects age-appropriate expectations for every child.

- Discuss times when a child with special needs cannot follow the established rules. Consider certain rules used at school and ask the child, "Would this rule be as easy for a person in a wheelchair, or a child who is blind, deaf, or has any other disability, to keep as it is for you to keep?" Discuss the role that the child might play in helping others to keep rules. For example, the child might retrieve items from a locker for a friend who is not as mobile.

- **Be firm, consistent, and fair.**
  - Once a rule is established, stick to it. Make sure rules are the same for all children. When a child sees a sibling or a classmate allowed to break a rule without consequences, it sends a message that rules vary with individuals. This creates a sense of injustice that may result in defiant behavior.

> "I generally avoid temptation unless I can't resist it."
> —Mae West

- **Provide experiences that teach children patience.** Part of learning self-control is learning to be patient.
  - Engage in activities that develop over time, such as planting seeds in a garden or working on a project using papier-mâché.
  - Discuss the joy of waiting and looking forward to something. Use classroom activities or events as examples—field trips, parent nights, carnivals, adopting a new pet, or planting and growing a vegetable garden. What are the small steps for each event that help build the joy and anticipation? If you are growing vegetables, you might make a schedule for caring for the plants, take pictures of plants as they grow, and plan a finished-product celebration in the kitchen.
  - Sitting still and waiting is not easy for any child. Encourage the child to brainstorm ideas for things he can do while waiting for lunch or for a turn on the playground. For example, sing songs, tell stories, play I Spy, make up names for the pigs in the story of "The Three Little Pigs," and so on.

- Ask the child to describe how waiting makes him feel. Suggest that he think of something he is looking forward to and ask him how looking forward to something makes him feel. Encourage the child to think of something he was looking forward to that has already happened. How did he feel when the event was over? It's not unusual to feel a little sad when an anticipated event is over. Sometimes remembering this helps us enjoy the waiting part a little more.
- Read books that are about anticipation, such as *Not Yet, Yvette* by Helen Ketteman, *Owl Moon* by Jane Yolen, *Leo the Late Bloomer* by Robert Kraus, and *I Can't Wait* by Elizabeth Crary. Discuss the circumstances in each story.

- **Discuss feelings (emotions) and ways to identify and handle them.**
  - Sing "If You're Surprised and You Know It" (page 101).
  - Use scenarios as springboards to discussion.
    - "Quinn just got a new bike. How do you think he feels? Why do you think he is happy?"
    - "Jeanne lost her favorite hair ribbon. How do you think she feels? Why?"
    - "Yolanda hurt her knee when she fell outside. How do you think she feels?"
    - "Trent hit his best friend. What do you think happened? It is ever alright to hit someone? How can we let people know we don't like something they do?"
  - Discuss explicit and inferred feeling of characters in literature.
    - "How do you think the little red hen felt when no one would help her?"
    - "How did Goldilocks feel when she woke up and saw the bears?"
    - "How did the bears feel when they found someone had entered their home without permission?"

- **Use natural and logical consequences for inappropriate behavior.**
  - Consequences are outcomes of behavior. They can be negative or positive. Consequences help shape future actions.
  - Natural consequences occur without outside control. For example, if a child refuses to wear his coat he will be cold. If you plant a flower and fail to water and care for it, it will die.
  - Logical consequences are determined by a person in authority and are reasonably connected to the behavior. For example, if Luis breaks the crayons, he will not be allowed to play with the crayons for a designated period of time. Logical and natural consequences help a child become

SEVEN SKILLS FOR SCHOOL SUCCESS

responsible for his behavior. Consequences are not punitive. They are instructional and intended to guide the child toward self-discipline.

● **Look beyond the behavior to the cause.**

 ● It is easy to become so focused on the behavior and fail to see the cause. According to Rudolf Dreikurs (2004), a trained physician and psychiatrist, there are four main causes or "mistaken goals" of misbehavior. These causes are attention, power, revenge, and the display of inadequacy. Dreikurs, along with many other modern educators, believe the true reason children misbehave is because they just "want to belong!"

 ● Use Rudolf Dreikurs' Goals of Misbehavior (see chart on the following page) to examine a defiant child. The chart states that the defiant child often feels that his world is somehow unfair. As an example, Mark is always in trouble. He knocks Adam's block structure down. He tears a page from a book. You find yourself constantly reprimanding him. When he gets in trouble he yells at you and accuses you of not liking him. What's going on? According to the chart, Mark's behavior indicates that he is defiant. When children get into a cycle of constantly being in trouble, they often feel that no one likes them because they don't like themselves. This becomes a vicious cycle if you don't stop to look beyond the behavior to the cause.

The Goals of Misbehavior

Goal	Child's Perspective	Adult Response	Strategies for Change
Attention	I'm only important when I am being noticed.	Annoyed	Ignore when possible Give unexpected attention Give attention to positive behavior
Power	I'm only important when I am in control.	Provoked Angry	Withdraw from conflict Redirect constructively when calm Establish equity
Defiance	No one likes me. I hurt. I feel better when I hurt others.	Hurt	Maintain order with minimum restraint Build trust Check for fairness Avoid retaliation
Display of inadequacy	I can't do anything right so I won't do anything at all.	Hopeless Discouraged	Be patient Encourage any effort Have faith in the child Refrain from pity or criticism

Adapted from *Discipline without Tears* by Rudolf Dreikurs, Pearl Cassel, and Eva Dreikurs-Ferguson.

● **Avoid over-stimulation.** Children are easily over stimulated because they are not as skilled as adults when it comes to focusing and maintaining attention (blocking out unimportant stimuli).
  ● Keep the environment uncluttered.
  ● Provide a quiet space for the child. Examples include a comfortable pile of pillows, a tent, or large appliance box stuffed with pillows.
  ● Balance active and passive activities. For example, after a stimulating outdoor play time, you might provide a quiet story time.

● **Offer limited choices.** Children have a difficult time making a choice when there are too many options. Limit choices to three. See page 48 for more information on choices.

- **Teach the Golden Rule:** "Do unto others as you want them to do unto you." Translation: Treat your friends as you would like to be treated.

- **Take time to train the behaviors you want to see.** If you reprimand the child without teaching him what the proper behavior is, he will continue to behave inappropriately.

Acknowledge Self-Control
- Catch the child doing something right and let him know you appreciate it when he follows the rules.
- Comment when the child uses his words to tell a friend how he feels.
- Ask the child who resolves a conflict to tell his friends how he did it.
- When you notice the child controlling his emotions, stop and ask him to tell you what he is feeling and how he is managing his feelings.

Reflect on Self-Control
- **Ask children questions that encourage them to think about self-control.**
   - What happens when you do something you aren't supposed to do?
   - How does breaking a toy hurt other people?
   - Why are there rules? What would happen if we didn't have rules?
   - What is the difference between doing what you want to do and doing what is the right thing to do? Can you think of a time you wanted to hit someone but used your words instead?

"Most powerful is he who has himself in his own power."
—*Seneca*

SEVEN SKILLS FOR SCHOOL SUCCESS

Relating to Others

5

WHAT IS RELATING TO OTHERS?

The act of being connected, related. (Adapted from Webster's II New College Dictionary)

Children who relate to others are comfortable in most social settings. They engage in conversation, offer input and opinions when asked, and are able to enter a pre-existing group with ease. Children who relate to others are capable of showing empathy.

A Child Shows Skills in Relating to Others When...	A Child Who Relates to Others Understands These Words...	
● She identifies and appropriately expresses feelings.	communicate	manners
● He assesses the feelings of others.	compromise	negotiate
● She relates to the feelings, motives, and concerns of others.	cooperate	relationship/s
	different	share
● He reads and responds to social cues.	empathy	similar
	feelings	tolerance
● She negotiates and resolves conflicts.	friend	unique
● He knows the difference between feeling and actions.	greet	
● She thinks creatively.		
● He acts cooperatively.		

WHY RELATING TO OTHERS MATTERS

Children's relationships with adults and peers provide a powerful social context that influences their behavior (Juvonen & Wentzel, 1996). Children observe and model the behaviors they see in others, especially those close to them. Children's families, friends outside of school, schools, neighborhoods, and culture also provide powerful contexts from which they will development their social skills and intelligence.

Children learn how to relate to one another and to adults by interacting with them. Children cannot learn what they need to become socially adept by interacting only with adults. Negotiating, sharing, and compromising are best learned from interactions with their peers.

Relating to others involves being able to read and appropriately respond to social cues. In order to be skilled at understanding others, children must be able to understand their own emotions and know how to express those emotions in appropriate ways. This insight is gained as children observe the adults and peers with whom they interact and as children put into practice the strategies they learn from their observations.

Language is a critical tool for relating to others. Words empower children to express themselves. Words allow children to have a base of power—the ability to enter group play, to resolve a conflict, to deal with sad or frightening experiences—to handle life.

Empathy

Researchers suggest that empathy is a critical social skill that is necessary for getting along with others. Empathy allows us to view a situation from someone else's point of view. In order for a child to be able to relate to another person's pleasure or pain, she must have experienced painful and pleasurable experiences.

Researchers say that children today are less likely to demonstrate empathy than children a few decades ago. One might say, "Empathy is intangible. How can it be measured?" Researchers use tangible elements (social trends) related to empathy as a means of determining the level of existence of empathy. The tangible elements are social trends that indicate a lack of empathy, such criminality, terrorism, decreased charity, violence, antisocial behavior, related mental-health disorders, and abuse. When these negative elements are on the rise, scientists extrapolate that empathy is on the decline. The chart on the following page provides data on the increase in several negative social trends.

"A friend is one who walks in when others walk out."
—Walter Winchell

Social Trend	Data
Violent Crimes Increase	Prisoners incarcerated for violent crimes doubles 1990—313,600 prisoners (violent crimes) 2007—687,700 prisoners (violent crimes) (Correctional populations in the US in 2007, Bureau of Justice Statistics http://www.ojp.usdoj.gov/bjs/prisons.htm)
Depression Increases	Increase in children between 7 and 17 years old suffering from depression 1995—1.44 million 2002—3.22 million (Gurian, 2007)
Use of Anti-Psychotic Drug Increases	Increases fivefold in 7 years from 1995 to 2002 1995—8.6 per 1,000 children 2005—40 per 1,000 children (Gurian, 2007) (The Associated Press, 2008) (http://www.msnbc.msn.com/id/11861986/)
Obesity Increases	2002 data showed that 15% of children and teens are considered overweight, a tripling since 1980. An additional 15% of kids and teens are considered "at risk" for becoming overweight. (http://www.americascores.org/index.php?id=390)
Child Abuse Increases	1995—43 per 1,000 children 2007—43.7 per 1,000 children (US Department of Human and Health Services) (http://www.acf.hhs.gov/programs/cb/stats_research/index.htm)

Tolerance

Relating to others requires tolerance—accepting customs, behaviors, beliefs, and appearances that are different from our own. Children learn tolerance as they experience interactions with others. The more children value variety, the more prepared they are to accept the differences of others. Children need interactions with others who are different in their abilities, appearances, and beliefs. From these experiences, children will become compassionate and accepting. When children are confident in their own uniquenesses, they are more accepting of the uniqueness of others.

Caring Communities

Caring communities foster a shared sense of responsibility, self-direction, and a strong motivation to learn where children develop social competence, respect for individual differences, and high expectations for themselves and others (Clark & Astuto, 1994; Lewis, Schaps, & Watson, 1996; Newmann, 1993). Caring communities are defined by Lewis, Schaps, and Watson as "places where teachers and students care about and support each other, actively participate in and contribute to activities and decisions, feel a sense of belonging and identification, and have a shared sense of purpose and common values." In a caring community of learners, children's emotional and intellectual development is nurtured through supportive relationships with adults. See the information in "Caring Communities of Learners: Five Interdependent Principles" on page 69 for a list of principles that provide a framework for communities of learners.

Caring Communities of Learners: Five Interdependent Principles

1. Warm, supportive, stable relationships. Children, teachers, staff, and parents are viewed as a team who work together for the optimal growth and development of all children.

2. Constructive learning. You can foster children's natural desire to understand their world by providing experiences that help children become more skillful, reflective, and self-evaluative in their learning. You can help children make discoveries, challenge them to find explanations, and encourage them to be tolerant of views different from their own.

3. An important, challenging curriculum that focuses on all areas of development: social, emotional, cognitive, and physical. The ultimate goal is to develop strong citizens.

4. Intrinsic motivation. Children are encouraged, not rewarded. Experiences are meaningful and children are helped to make personal connections to what they are learning.

5. Attention is given to social and ethical dimensions of learning. Children are taught to be responsible for their learning and for their behavior. Collaborative and cooperative approaches are used for problem solving and for conflict resolution.

Adapted from Lewis, C., Schaps, E., & Watson, M. (1996, September). "The Caring Classrooms' Academic Edge." *Educational Leadership*, pp. 16-21.

WHAT THE RESEARCH SAYS
- Babies are wired for social intelligence beginning at birth.
- The window of opportunity for wiring cooperative behavior is between the 24th and 48th month.
- Scientists suggest that the more active a person's mirror neuron system, the stronger her capacity for empathy.

(Ramey & Ramey, 1999; Ramey & Ramey, 1999; Goleman, 2006)

Relating to Others

WHAT YOU CAN DO TO BOOST A CHILD'S SKILLS IN RELATING TO OTHERS

Model Relating to Others

- **Pay attention to children's facial expressions and body language.** Say to the child, "You look happy today. What's going on?" or "I could tell by your eyes that it surprised you when Joseph handed you the ball."

- **Express your feelings when appropriate.** Children will learn that feelings are a natural part of life.
  - If you get frustrated because it is raining outside, you might say, "I feel frustrated because it's raining. I wanted to spend time outdoors today."
  - When something makes you happy let the child know. "I am so happy. You put your coat on all by yourself. See my smile."
  - "I feel sad that you kicked me. Let's think of another way you could tell me you don't want to clean up."

- **Express your joy at having a variety of items to choose from.** Tolerance is based, in part, on embracing variety.

- **Show your sadness when someone is hurt or feeling sick.**

Talk About Relating to Others

- **There are several children's books that provide a springboard for discussing feelings:** *Miss Tizzy* by Libba Moore Gray (feeling sad), *Chester's Way* by Kevin Henkes (feeling left out), *Matthew and Tillie* by Rebecca Jones (feeling angry), and *Swimmy* by Leo Lionni (feeling frightened) are just a few.

- **Ask open-ended questions during and after a story to encourage children to reflect.** Help the child connect her feelings to the feelings of the character in the story. For example, in *Swimmy* by Leo Lionni, Swimmy loses all his friends when a big fish eats them. Ask, "How do you think Swimmy felt when he lost his friends?" Swimmy has to find the courage to swim again. "When you have courage, does it mean you are not afraid? Can you remember a time when you felt frightened?"

- **Read books that relate to friendship.** For example, in *Matthew and Tilly* by Rebecca Jones, Matthew accidentally breaks Tilly's crayon and she gets angry and says some really mean things to him. Ask, "How do you think Matthew felt?" or "Have you ever been angry with a friend? What did you do?" Discuss things that cause friends to become angry. Discuss why friends forgive each other. Here are other books with themes related to friendship and getting along with others.

Accept and Value Each Person by Cheri Meiners
Amos and Boris by William Steig
Best Friends by Steven Kellogg
Chester's Way by Kevin Henkes
Chrysanthemum by Kevin Henkes
The Doorbell Rang by Pat Hutchinson
Frog and Toad Together by Arnold Lobel
How to Be a Friend by Lauren Krasny Brown
Hurray for Pre-K! by Ellen B. Senisi
Join In and Play by Cheri Meiners
The Lion and the Mouse (Aesop fable)
Matthew and Tilly by Rebecca Jones
Miss Tizzy by Libba Moore Gray
Old Henry by Joan Blos
Swimmy by Leo Lionni
That's What Friends Are For by Florence Parry Heide
That's What Friends Do by Kathryn Cave

- **Encourage children to talk about their feelings and listen intently to what they have to say.** Maintain eye contact with the child. Paraphrase what she says and help her sort through her thoughts and ideas. Vivian Paley, author of *The Kindness of Children* (1999), says that although each child comes into the world with an instinct for kindness, it is a lesson that must be reinforced at every turn. Paley suggests that conversations about kindness, fairness, and justice need to happen well before children enter elementary school.

● **Create scenarios describing accidents that might happen with another child.** Ask the child to describe what she would do or say if the accident happened to her.

Incident	Appropriate Response
Ashley spilled her juice and it got on Brianna's dress.	"I'm sorry. I will get something to help dry you off."
Ivan tripped on a block and accidentally knocked Paul's building down.	"I'm sorry. I will help you rebuild it."
Austin throws the ball and it hits another child.	"I'm sorry. I was trying to throw the ball in the box. Are you okay?"

● Ask feeling questions. "How would you feel if...
  ● You were the librarian and people took books out of your library without signing them out?
  ● You were the playground helper and your friends didn't help you bring in the play equipment?
  ● You let your friend play with your favorite truck and he broke it?
  ● You were trying to go to sleep and your friends kept making loud noises?
  ● You were going down the slide and other children kept trying to climb up?

● Describe scenarios that elicit emotional reactions. Ask the child to describe the emotions she might feel in each situation.

Situation	Possible Reactions
Someone accuses you of something you didn't do.	Angry, sad
You receive a puppy for a birthday present.	Happy, surprised
Your best friend is not feeling well and couldn't go to school with you.	Sad, lonely
A friend snatched a book from you.	Angry, frustrated
Someone tells you that you look nice.	Pleased, happy

- **Watch for a "teachable moment" to discuss empathy.** For example, if a child's friend falls down on the playground and no one notices, involve the child in caring for her friend. If the child is having a difficult time working a puzzle and no one notices, ask another child to help her finish the puzzle. Help the child remember what it feels like to fall or what it feels like to have a tough time doing something that is challenging for you.

- **Read books with content that explicitly relates to empathy** such as *Understand and Care* by Cheri Meiners and *When I Care About Others* by Cornelia Maude Spelman. Discuss the stories. Point out the parts of the story where someone expresses care and concern for how someone else feels. Other books with empathy themes are *Miss Tizzy* by Libba Moore Gray and *Old Henry* by Joan Blos.

- **Talk about tolerance.** Being tolerant means that we don't judge people who are different in some way—in opinion, practice, appearance, beliefs, or customs. Discuss similarities and differences in friends. Some children are taller than others. Some have dark hair while others have light hair. Eyes and skin are often different colors. Incorporate activities that focus on identifying similarities and differences.

Practice Relating to Others

- **When a child expresses an emotion, use the opportunity to teach about that emotion.**
  - "You're feeling frustrated right now because we have to go inside."
  - "It surprised you to see how happy Kathy is to share her crayons."
  - "I can see you are angry because Sam got to the tricycle ahead of you. Remember yesterday Linda was angry because you beat her to the tricycle."

- **Show children photos of people who are expressing emotions.** Ask questions about the photos. "What do you think the man is feeling? How can you tell? What do you think might have made him angry?"

"A friend is someone who is there for you when he'd rather be anywhere else."
—Len Wein

- **Sing songs about emotions.** "If You're Surprised and You Know It" (fourth verse of "If You're Happy and You Know It" on page 101) helps the child learn appropriate ways to express emotions. Encourage the child to add other verses or describe other appropriate ways to express the emotions used in the verses of the song. See pages 101–102 for other songs about emotions.

- **Teach basic rules of politeness.**
  - "Please" and "thank you" are usually the first "manners words" children acquire. Use "please" and "thank you" appropriately and expect the child to use these words.
  - Teach the child to say "hello" when friends arrive and "goodbye" when they leave. Set an example by saying, "hello" and "goodbye" to all who come and go.
  - Discuss sharing, taking turns, and paying attention when others speak.
  - Forcing the child to say "I'm sorry" doesn't teach empathy or manners. A superficial "I'm sorry" is worse than saying nothing. Make sure that the child knows "I'm sorry" is an appropriate thing to say when she has hurt someone or broken a rule, but let her decide if she wishes to say it.
  - Read books about being polite, such as *Be Polite and Kind* by Cheri Meiners, *Manners Can Be Fun* by Munro Leaf, *This Little Piggy's Book of Manners* by Kathryn Madeline Allen, or *Respect and Take Care of Things* by Cheri Meiners.

- **Teach children to greet each other in different languages.** This will help the child to feel "smart," knowing how to say "hello" in several languages.

Language	Greeting
Spanish	Hola *or* Buenos dias
French	Bon jour
Hawaiian	Aloha
Russian	Zdravstvuite (ZzDRAST-vet-yah)
German	Guten Tag (GOOT-en Tahk)

"A friend is someone who knows the song in your heart, and can sing it back to you when you have forgotten the words."
—Anonymous

● **Teach visual and verbal clues.**

- Children often have trouble understanding that different tones of voice signal different emotional cues. Choose a phrase and say it over and over in different tones of voice that would represent different feelings. For example, you might say "listen" in a light, happy voice to indicate you have exciting news to share. You might say "listen" in a stern voice indicating you are angry. You might say "listen" in a whisper to suggest something important is going to be said.

- Ask the child questions about how she can figure out how people are feeling by what people say or do.
  - "What do we say when we are happy?" ("Hooray," "Yippee," "Wow!" "Hot dog!")
  - "How do you know when someone is sad?" (They cry. They don't smile. They say, "I'm sad.")
  - "How do you know if someone is angry without them telling you?" (They stomp their feet. They yell. They hit or shove.) "When you are angry, how do you let your friends know?"

● **Teach strategies for negotiating and resolving conflicts.** See pages 32–33 for suggestions regarding problem solving. See pages 92–94 for cooperative games.

● **Teach empathy clearly and directly.**

- Stay cognizant of "teachable moment" opportunities for modeling and teaching empathy. When two or more children are playing and one gets hurt, involve the others in caring for the hurt friend. Discuss what can be done to "fix the hurt" and remind those helping what it feels like to be hurt. Involve children in charitable opportunities, such as collecting toys for children at Christmas or food at Thanksgiving, visiting a non-contagious sick friend, or making a get-well card for a relative.

- Use situations that occur with other children or animals to teach about feelings (emotions).
  - Help the child care for a pet. Ask questions. "How do you think your guinea pig feels when it is alone during the night? How do you think it feels when it sees you in the morning? What does your dog do when you

come home? What do you think wagging his tail and barking means? What do you think your dog is trying to communicate when he whimpers?"

- "What could a friend say that would make you feel angry? sad? happy? surprised? or worried?"

- Teach the child that all living creatures have a right to life. If the child is killing caterpillars, talk with her about the fact that caterpillars are living creatures with a right to live and a contribution to make to the earth. Read books about being kind to animals, such as *Tails Are Not for Pulling* by Elizabeth Verdick, *Pets Have Feelings Too* by Monica Diedrich, or *Do Animals Have Feelings Too?* by David L. Rice and Trudy Calvert.

- Acknowledge empathy when you see it used. "That was kind of you to let Chris have your car. You could see he was upset. Look at him. He's smiling now."

- Make greeting cards, draw pictures, or collect books for children in the hospital. Visit the children if acceptable.

- Visit the elderly in a senior home. Sing songs for them.

- **Explicitly teach tolerance.**
  - Celebrate differences. Make a graph of colors of crayons, shapes of blocks, or types of cookies.
  - Display items from cultures and countries around the world.
  - Communicate with pen pals from other countries.
  - List the characteristics of characters in stories. Make a diagram to show how the characters are similar and how they are different.
  - Embrace variety. Offer a variety of writing utensils, blocks, types of cars, books, dress-up clothing, types of art paper, and so on.
  - Facilitate interactions between with children who have special needs and typically developing children. Children benefit from interactions with peers who have mobility issues (such as a child in a wheelchair), children with hearing losses, and children who have attention deficit disorder.

- **Plan interactions with people of all ages.** Offer experiences that help the child become familiar with people of all ages. Visit babies. Talk about what babies are learning. "What do you think it feels like to be unable to talk?" "What does it feel like to have to depend on someone to move you from place to place because you can't walk?" Visit a senior citizen home. Ask appropriate questions. "Do you think the people we visited enjoyed having us as guests?"

- **Teach children games that two or more children can play together.**
  - Play Don't Let the Ball Fall. Give two children a ball and have them toss it into the air and then try to keep it aloft.
  - Make Partner Ice Cream (see Appendix page 109).
  - Blow bubbles and have children attempt to keep the bubbles aloft. Let one child blow the bubbles while the second child chases the bubbles.
  - Invite two children to play Tic-Tac-Toe.
  - Play Pair, Think, and Share. Have two children work together to form an alphabet letter using their bodies.
  - Play cooperation games, such as Cooperative Musical Chairs, Back-to-Back Lifts, Tummy Ticklers, and Cover the Square. See pages 92–94 for directions.
  - Play Elbow Cut-Ins with a group of children. Select a child to be IT. Have each of the remaining children find a partner. Instruct partners to hook elbows. Count to three as a signal for partners to start running. IT catches up with one of the pairs and hooks elbows with one of the two children. The other child becomes the new IT. She must join herself to another pair.

- **Develop a vocabulary about emotions and actions.** A common vocabulary is conducive to helping the child communicate her emotions and actions. Work on teaching social words that will help her be on an equal playing field as she begins to interact with others. Words like "please," "thank you," "take turns," "share," "cooperate," and "feel" will all be used as she navigates her way through group play and interactions.

- **Teach children about random acts of kindness.** Help the child find things she can do that will help others. Perhaps she might bake cookies for a senior citizen home, decorate the door of a neighbor, or surprise a friend with a bouquet of wildflowers.

> "Don't walk in front of me, I may not follow. Don't walk behind me, I may not lead. Walk beside me and be my friend."
> —Albert Camus
> (also attributed to Maimonidies)

Acknowledge Relating to Others

- **Comment on children's friendships.** Talk about what friends enjoy about each other.

- **Notice children who display empathy and compassion.** Say, "It feels nice when we care for others."

- **Add your support to children who are cheering for or encouraging a friend.** For example, if you see the child trying to teach a friend how to roll a playdough snake, add your support and, perhaps, a suggestion or two.

- **Ask children to describe their problem-solving ideas.** Invite the child who works out a problem, such as sharing a bicycle or deciding who goes first down the slide, to describe how she resolved her problem.

- **Recognize children who help others.** If you see the child helping a friend, comment on what she is doing to help.

- **Teach children to cheer for the accomplishments of their friends.** Encourage the child to clap when her friend jumps a long distance or lands the beanbag inside the basket.

Reflect on Relating to Others
- **Ask children questions that encourage them to think about relationships.**
  - What does it mean to be a friend?
  - How do you show your friends you care about them?
  - What should you do when a friend gets hurt?
  - How do you feel when someone snatches something from your hand? What should you say when this happens?
  - How do you let your friends know that you want to participate in their game?

"The glory of friendship is not in the outstretched hand, nor the kindly smile, nor the joy of companionship; it is in the spiritual inspiration that comes to one when he discovers that someone else believes in him and is willing to trust him."
—*Ralph Waldo Emerson*

Communication

6

WHAT IS THE CAPACITY TO COMMUNICATE?

A process by which information is exchanged between individuals through a common system of symbols, signs, or behavior. (Adapted from Webster's II New College Dictionary)

Children who are capable communicators are able to clearly express their needs and wants. They are able to engage with others in a meaningful dialogue.

A Child Shows the Ability to Communicate When...	A Communicative Child Understands These Words...	
• She expresses thoughts clearly.	communicate	information
• He solicits help from adults when needed.	contribute	read
• She expresses emotions appropriately.	describe	share
• He participates in group activities.	expand	talk
• She reads and responds to social cues.	express	trust
• He uses words to resolve conflict.	feelings	write
• She answers questions when asked.	help	
• He offers information during group discussion.		
• She greets peers and adults appropriately.		

WHY COMMUNICATION MATTERS

So much depends on effective communication. When you are unable to communicate clearly and effectively, the result can be disastrous—the cause of war, the end of a marriage, the loss of a job, the end of a friendship.

Good communication includes listening, questioning, understanding, and responding to what is being communicated. It is important to be able to communicate individually and within a group. Effective communication is a two-way process.

Communication is not just about the words that people use, but also the manner of speaking, body language and, above all, the effectiveness with which we listen. Knowing how to listen to people makes them feel valued and involved.

"Self-expression must pass into communication for its fulfillment."

—Pearl S. Buck

Being "Fully Present"

Oral communication is a two-way street of listening and speaking. Listening is as important as speaking. We need to be "fully present" when we listen to anyone speak. This means we need to listen with all our senses. Being "fully present" requires thinking throughout the day instead of simply moving through the day. Being "fully present" means being sensitive and not self-absorbed or task-absorbed.

When you are "fully present" you are cognizant of the child who is standing alone watching others play a game. You notice the heavy sighs of a child who tries again and again to tie his shoe. You take the time to listen and respond to a child's needs when a child shows you his artwork or something he built with blocks. Being "fully present" means at that moment nothing is more important than listening and interacting with the child.

Being "fully present" means living in the moment and taking your relationships with others seriously. Being "fully present" happens in all realms of life. A horse trainer is "fully present" when he takes a quick survey of the area around him when his horse stops short and refuses to move. The trainer senses that the horse is afraid and instead of prodding him on, he takes a moment to try to understand the significance of the stop. He notices the "new thing" (a plastic sack) in the area that has caused his horse to stop. He allows the horse to get used to the sack by sniffing it and walking around it before he nudges him forward. Being sensitive and aware is communicating "between the lines."

Pre-Wired to Speak

Humans are born biologically prepared to speak. The only thing our brains need to be wired for language is someone speaking to us. Communication, however, is a learned process. We depend on others to guide us through experiences that will allow us to learn the nuances of interacting verbally with others.

Babies begin to interact socially the moment they make eye contact with their parents and caretakers. Their understanding of social cues is clear after only a few weeks, when we smile and they smile back. Speaking skills are also taking root. Babies listen carefully to the sounds of spoken words. After a few weeks, babies begin to babble and coo, showing they are beginning to grasp the concept of spoken language. They will even attempt a give-and-take conversation of cooing. We speak, and when we stop babies begin to coo, responding to our words. By six months, babies begin to put the sounds of language into the form of syllables like "ma, ma, ma" and "da, da, da." This is not "mommy" and "daddy". It is simply the blending of sounds.

Around the age of one, vocabulary begins to develop and the baby points to his mother and says, "ma-ma" or daddy and says, "da-da." During the second year of life, little ones acquire many vocabulary words and even begin to put a few of those words together to form sentences. Between two and three years of age, the sentences grow from simple to more complex. Children begin to pick up the nuances of language structure and syntax. They learn when to add "ed" to verbs, when to drop the "s" from nouns, and when to add the "s" to nouns. It will take four years before they complete the journey of learning to speak, but what a marvelous journey it is!

Speaking with Purpose

An important extension of language acquisition is the use of language for specific purposes. One of those purposes is to help navigate the social world. Children learn to use their words to express their emotions, to get their needs met, to negotiate a position in play, to interact with their friends, to participate in group discussions, and more.

Social Etiquette

Communication skills include knowledge of verbal etiquette. Social interactions require us to offer an appropriate greeting, respond politely when someone asks a question or gives a gift, say "thank you" when someone compliments us, and "please" when we ask someone else to do us a favor. Verbal etiquette is learned from watching the interactions of those around us and from practicing the correct addresses and responses as situations arise.

The ability to communicate is at the heart of social and emotional intelligence. Children who master communication skills move effortlessly through school and through life.

WHAT THE RESEARCH SAYS

- Vocabulary begins to wire in the brain from birth. By the time children are 18 months old, those who have been around chatty adults will have 181 more vocabulary words than those who were not around chatty adults. By the age of two, the gap has grown to 295 words. This head start will stay with children for their entire lifetime.
- Early sounds wire in the brain during the first year of life between the fourth and eighth months. Neural communities (pathways) will be forged for every sound in the child's native language. For English, that will be 44 networks.

(Family and Work Institute, 1996; Nash, 1997)
(Nash, 1997; Ramey & Ramey, 1999)
(Snow, Catherine (2005) "From Literacy to Learning." Harvard Education Letter (July/August) Online: www.edletter.org/current/snow.shtml.)

WHAT YOU CAN DO TO BOOST A CHILD'S COMMUNICATION SKILLS

Model Communication

- **Use proper grammar.** Children imitate what they hear.

- **Model verbal etiquette.** Say, "please" and "thank you" as you interact with children and with others. Begin every morning with "Good morning!"

- Use vocabulary that shows compassion and empathy. When someone is upset, talk about it. For example, say, "How do you think that makes him feel?" "I bet he is sad that he has to leave in the middle of his game. How can we tell he is sad?" "Have you ever had to quit something in the middle? How did you feel?" (See pages 72–76 for information on teaching empathy.)

- **Introduce interesting words, such as "peculiar," "spectacular," "absurd," "rhombus," and so on.** If you use a word several times, you will be surprised how quickly a child learns how to use it, too.

- **Use complete sentences and expect children to do the same.** Instead of saying, "Hurry," say, "Let's move quickly."

- **Use descriptive vocabulary.** The more attributes you put in a sentence, the clearer the sentence is to the listener.

- **Be "fully present."** Listen to the child with all of your senses so he learns to do the same.

Talk About Communication

- **Discuss and demonstrate how directions can be unclear when the speaker doesn't provide enough information.** For example, if you say, "Bring me the ball," it may be difficult for the child to know which ball you want. If you say, "Bring me the small orange-and-blue striped ball" it is clear which ball you are referring to.

- **Talk about manners.** Why do we have them? When do we use them? Read some of Cheri Meiners' manners books, *Share and Take Turns* or *Be Polite and Kind*.

- **Read books with a communication theme.** Use stories as a springboard to communication. For example, *Marti and the Mango* by Daniel Moreton is about a mouse that is looking for a mango, but it uses insufficient information. You can use this book to discuss descriptive words. Use *The King Who Rained* by Fred Gwynne to discuss words that have more than one meaning. Here are some other books with communication themes:

> "Feelings of worth can flourish only in an atmosphere where individual differences are appreciated, mistakes are tolerated, communication is open, and rules are flexible—the kind of atmosphere that is found in a nurturing family."
>
> —*Virginia Satir*

The Blind Men and the Elephant by Karen Backstein

Dear Mr. Blueberry by Simon James

The Emperor's New Clothes (many versions available)

Epossumondas by Coleen Salley

The Gardener by Sarah Stewart

Henny Penny (many versions available)

*Julius Anteater, Misunderstoo*d by Lynn Rowe Reed

The Old Man and the Door by Gary Soto

Tops and Bottoms by Janet Stevens

Practice Communication

- **Build trust.** Trust is the act of placing yourself in the vulnerable position of relying on others to treat you in a fair, open, and honest way. Trust is the foundation of relationships. Until children trust you, they will probably keep most things and feelings from you.
  - Create rules. Start with one or two simple rules. Allow the child to help set the rules. Discuss the reasons for rules and the consequences of obeying the rules and the consequences of breaking the rules.
  - Listen to the child when he speaks—even when it takes him a long time to communicate his ideas. Remember, all children are on a continuum, moving from a completely non-verbal state to a very verbal state, which they will achieve with your help and guidance.
  - Give the child responsibilities. This builds a sense of partnership and ownership.
  - Use words that build trust such as "we," "us," "friends," "sharing," "caring," and so on.

- **Help children fall in love with language.** When children play with language they develop a sense of rhythm and meter that will give them a better understanding of intonation and expression. Playing with language also builds a desire to explore language to its fullest extent.
  - Encourage the child to play with rhyming words. Demonstrate making nonsense rhymes like "ooey, gooey, tooey, mooey." Let him create a rhyming word to go with his name.
  - Teach the child onomatopoeia words (words that sound like the sound they are trying to describe). Sing songs like "The Wheels on the Bus" and "Old MacDonald Had a Farm." Point out the onomatopoetic words.
  - Teach the child tongue twisters.
  - Read books with rhyming word passages, such Dr. Suess books and nursery rhymes. Read books with predictable language patterns. Read poetry and prose.

● **Listen with interest. Be "fully present."**

- Always talk with the child at his eye level. Look him in the eyes when he is speaking. Listen only to what he is saying. Repeat his questions or statements back for clarity. If appropriate, place your hands on his shoulders or forearms. If he has asked you a question, ask for his answer before you offer your answer. You will be surprised how much you will find out about the child if you just take a moment and really listen to what he says.

- Listen to sounds that might indicate something out of kilter, such as a raised voice, a heavy sigh, a moan, and so on.

- Stop everything when a child asks you a question or makes a statement directly to you. Listen with all your senses to his words and respond appropriately.

● **Expand children's vocabulary.**

- Mentally review songs before you sing them. Is there vocabulary in the song that the child might not understand? Does he know what the waterspout is in "Itsy Bitsy Spider" (page 100)? Does he know what the word "peculiar" means in "Catalina Magnalina" (page 106)? Discuss words in songs that may be unfamiliar.

- Change words in songs to create new vocabulary. For example, you might sing "This old man, he played a flute, made it hum and made it toot," instead of "This old man he played one…" (page 107). When singing "Twinkle, Twinkle, Little Star," change the word "little" to other adjectives—"tiny," "gigantic," or "silent." Change your voice to match the adjective.

- Review stories before you read them. Identify words that may be unfamiliar to the child. Introduce the words before reading the story.

- Introduce five new vocabulary words each week. Use the words each day. Encourage the child to use the words. Acknowledge when the child uses the new words by having him place a button in a jar or a check mark beside the word he used. Make up games that center around using the new words. For example, you might have the child make up a sentence using one of the words. Challenge him to get two of the new words in one sentence.

- Use photo cards, such as *The Infant and Toddler Photo Activity* Cards or *The Preschool Photo Activity Cards* published by Gryphon House, to stimulate vocabulary and language. An effective set of cards will have interesting, yet simple, photographs with helpful suggestions for you on the back of the card.

- Invite the child to describe a new toy or an item found in the yard. Treat the conversation as if the child is giving a report. Ask the questions. For example, "Where did you get the acorn? When did you first see it? What will you do with it?"

- **Encourage appropriate language.**
  - When the child uses inappropriate grammar, simply repeat his sentence, inserting the appropriate language.
  - Do not accept "baby talk." Ask the child to repeat what he said in a more understandable voice.
  - Encourage a "whisperer" to speak louder. Remind him that you cannot help him if you cannot hear him. If you respond to whispers, you prolong the amount of time it takes to get the child to speak up.

- **Use sign language as a bridge to oral language.** This works well with reluctant speakers or second-language speakers. Sign language is an effective way to communicate. Here is a great song to teach a few signs.

Sign Along with Me by Pam Schiller
(Tune: "Mary Had a Little Lamb")
This is please and this is thank you.
This is please. This is thank you.
This is please and this is thank you.
Sign along with me.

Other verses:
  Up and down
  More and stop

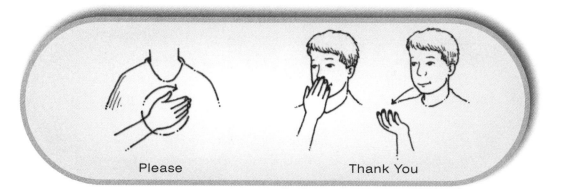
Please   Thank You

● **Teach children the purposes of written communication.**
  - Have the child write thank-you notes.
  - Write letters to pen pals. Exchange notes with someone from another city or state.
  - Help the child brainstorm a list of things that are necessary for taking care of a pet, things he might hear on a listening walk, or things that start with a specific letter of the alphabet.
  - Suggest that the child write or dictate stories that are based on the books you read to him.
  - Collect environmental print and create a display for it. How many things can the child read?

● **Practice conversation.**
  - Engage the child in conversations. Ask about the picture he is drawing. Ask him to describe how he built the highway with blocks. "Where is your highway going?"
  - Make a set of conversation starter cards (see page 113). Use the cards to stimulate conversation or use them to play a game.

Acknowledge Communication

● **Comment on children's ability to communicate their ideas clearly.** "That was very clear. I knew exactly what you were asking me to do."

● **When the child learns a new vocabulary word, write it down** and ask the child to say what the word means. Try to use the new word several times during the day.

● **Pair children with mature language skills with those whose skills are less advanced.** Pair the child with a second-language learner. Allow the child to act as an interpreter but remind him that he is also a teacher so he should not speak for the other person, just assist that person where necessary. Children often learn more easily from their peers than from adults.

● **Celebrate as children extend their language capabilities.** Let the child know that you can tell he is improving.

"When people talk, listen completely. Most people never listen."
—*Ernest Hemingway*

Reflect on Communication

● **Ask children questions that encourage them to think about communication skills.**

  ● What happens when you ask for something but don't describe it very well?
  ● What happens when you don't receive clear directions?
  ● How can you communicate with someone who doesn't speak the same language that you speak?
  ● Why is communication important?
  ● How would you know what other people were thinking if they were not able to tell you with words?
  ● How do you use written language?

7

Cooperativeness

WHAT IS COOPERATIVENESS?

A willingness and ability to work with others. (Adapted from Webster's II New College Dictionary)

Children who are cooperative are team players. They are helpful. They focus on problem solving as a means of bringing about mutually acceptable outcomes.

A Child Shows Cooperativeness When...	A Cooperative Child Understands These Words...	
• He shares toys and materials with others without being asked to do so.	commitment	partner
• She takes turns.	depend	sharing
• He participates in problem-solving activities.	friends	team
• She relates to the feelings, motives, and concerns of others.	group	together
• He reads and responds to social cues.	helping	work
• She negotiates and resolves conflicts with others.	others	
• He thinks creatively.		

Why Cooperativeness Matters

Cooperation is at the heart of an organized society. Without cooperative effort, things would be chaotic. Imagine a culture where no one obeys the rules, or a neighborhood where everyone is responsible for hauling their own trash to the dump, or where houses can be made of anything and families keep any hours they wish.

Cooperation allows us to work toward common goals. It functions with law and order to create an organized society. With cooperation, we accomplish tasks more quickly and easily than by working alone. Sometimes we need the support of others to accomplish our goals. We are often stronger together than we might be alone. (See the Aesop fable of "The Farmer and His Quarrelsome Sons" in the box on this page).

The Farmer and His Quarrelsome Sons—An Aesop Fable About Cooperation

A farmer asked his quarrelsome sons to place a bunch of sticks before him. After his sons placed the sticks before him, the farmer bound the sticks together and challenged his sons, one after one, to pick up the bundle of sticks and break them.

They all tried, but in vain. Then the farmer untied the bundle and gave the sons the sticks to break one by one. They did this with the greatest of ease. Then the father said, "Remember, my sons, as long as you remain united, you are a match for anything, but differ and separate, and you are undone."

Moral: *There is strength in unity.*

Capacity for cooperative behavior wires in the brain between the 24th and 48th months of life. Like all other neural circuitry, cooperative behavior is forged by experience. Play begins as solitary play—babies play by themselves. During the second year of life, toddlers begin to play beside other children. By age three, children play beside a friend and interact occasionally with a word here or there. These interactions become more involved as children move into cooperative play during the third year. In cooperative play, interactions become meaningful and purposeful.

Children between the ages of two and four need social contacts so they can experience social interactions. They will learn to share, negotiate, take turns, and resolve conflicts. The quality and quantity of their experiences will, to a large degree, influence their social intelligence. Children need experiences with their peers so that their learning occurs on a level playing field. During group play, children receive immediate social feedback from their peers. This information becomes a powerful tool that children can use to construct their knowledge of social nuances. Children are not able to learn everything they need to know about cooperative behavior from an adult because adults always have more power and a far greater amount of experience.

WHAT THE RESEARCH SAYS

- The window of opportunity for wiring cooperative behavior is between the 24th and 48th months of life.
- When we feel valued and cared for, as we might when engaged in cooperative experiences, the brain releases the neurotransmitters of pleasure: endorphins and dopamine. Pleasure is a strong motivator in shaping our behaviors.
- Cooperative projects engage emotions. Emotions increase attention, create meaning, and enhance memory.
  (Epstein, 2007; Jensen, 2005; Caine, et al, 2008)

"Great discoveries and improvements invariably involve the cooperation of many minds."
—Alexander Graham Bell

Model Cooperativeness

- **Lend a helping hand.** Remember that a picture is worth a thousand words. Model helping others.

- **Integrate yourself into children's play.** Sit down and help build a fort, join a tea party, help work through an experiment or be a player in a game. As you interact with the child, discuss the value of working together on a project. You have two people thinking, two people working, and two people sharing the joy of completion.

Talk About Cooperativeness

- **Discuss things you do that require cooperation,** such as playing in a bowling league, participating in a book club, or sharing transportation in a car pool. Explain how the cooperation makes the activity/situation better.

- **Show children photos of people working together.** Use the photos as springboards to discussion.

- **Talk about things that run more smoothly because people cooperate.** For example, everyone helps during clean-up time so that it goes more smoothly and quickly. Children take turns in centers so that no center has too many children for the number of toys in the center. At home, the family works together to keep the house neat. Each person picks up her own mess.

- **Read books that are related to cooperation.** For example, in *Swimmy* by Leo Lionni, the small fish swim together to appear larger so they won't be eaten by the bigger fish. Who thought of this idea? Was it a good plan? Discuss how things work better when everyone works together. Here are some other books that relate to cooperation:

> *The Blind Men and the Elephant* by Karen Backstein
> *Eight Animals Bake a Cake* by Susan Middleton Elya
> *Fox Tale Soup* by Tony Bonning
> *The Great Big Enormous Turnip* by Alexei Tolstoy
> *The Little Red Hen* (traditional, many versions available)
> *Pitch In!* by Pamela Hill Nettleton
> *Stone Soup* by Heather Forest
> *Swimmy* by Leo Lionni
> *That's What Friends Are For* by Florence Parry Heide
> *Where Is the Leopard? A Tale of Cooperation* by Wendy Wax

We may have all come on different ships, but we're in the same boat now.

—*Martin Luther King, Jr.*

Practice Cooperation

- **Play games that promote a cooperative effort.**
  - *Cooperative Musical Chairs:* This game is a variation of Musical Chairs. Make a circle on the floor with masking tape. Play a piece of music. Encourage children to walk around the circle until the music stops. When the music stops, everyone steps into the circle. The idea is to get everyone inside so everyone wins. Continue playing for as long as children are interested.
  - *Tummy Ticklers:* Have children lie on the floor on their backs with their heads on someone else's tummy. Do something silly to make children start laughing. What is making their heads jiggle? This activity should cause contagious laughing. Help children see the cooperative results of their laughing.
  - *Cover the Square:* Place a 12" x 12" square of paper on the floor. Give each child a beanbag and have her toss her beanbag onto the square, with the ultimate goal being to completely cover the square with the beanbags. Everyone's bag and good aim is needed. Let those who miss the first time try again until their beanbags land on the square. Do children notice that it is

better when they have a plan? If everyone tosses their bags at one time, what happens?

- *Pass the Potato:* Give each child a spoon. Have all the children stand in a line. Place a potato in the spoon of the child at the front of the line. Challenge the children to pass the potato spoon to spoon down the line. Can they pass the potato to the end of the line without dropping it?

- *Pass the Cup:* Have the children form a line beside an empty bucket. Give the child at the far end of the line a cup of water and instruct her to pass it to the friend beside her. Have the children pass the cup until they reach the end of the line. Have the last child pour the water into the bucket. Start another cup down the line. How many cups does it take to fill the bucket? What happens if someone spills the water?

- *Tug of Peace:* Take hula hoops outdoors and encourage children to play the Tug of Peace game. It takes cooperative effort. Children sit around the hula hoop and grab hold with both hands. By pulling back on the hoop, can everyone stand up together?

- *Loud and Soft Hide and Seek:* Select a child to be IT. Ask IT to leave the room. Hide a beanbag. When IT returns, tell her that you and the children are going to sing a song while she looks for the beanbag. When she is close to where the beanbag is hidden, sing louder. When she moves farther away, sing softly.

- *Musical Freeze:* Invite the children to hold hands and dance or move in a circle while a favorite song plays. Tell the children that when the music stops they are to freeze as a group. When you start the music again, they can move again.

- *Calliope Fun:* Divide children into four groups. Instruct group one to make sound #1, group two to make sound #2, and group three to make sound #3, group four will hum the circus song (the song you generally hear on a merry-go-round).
  Sound #1: *Um pa pa, um pa pa…*
  Sound #2: *Um tweedli-dee, um tweedli-dee…*
  Sound #3: *Um shhh, um shhh, um shhh…*

- *Through the Hoop:* Have the children make a straight line holding hands. Without letting go at any time, the object is to move a hoop from one end of the line, passing each child through it. If someone lets go, return the hoop to the beginning.

- *Cat and Mouse:* You need two balls, one larger than the other; Nerf balls work well. Seat children in a circle.

Tell a short story about how the cat always chases the mouse but the mouse is little and quick so she always gets away. Hand the balls to one of children starting with the small ball and then adding the larger ball. The idea is to pass the balls around the circle quickly without letting the big ball get ahead of the small ball.

- *Shadow Creations:* On a sunny day take the children outdoors. Challenge them to make shadows with different characteristics, such as shadows that are tall, skinny, small, and so on. Have the children work in pairs to create interesting shadow shapes, such as monsters, machines, animals, giants, and so on.

- *Bubble Bump:* Divide the children into groups of three. Instruct each group to join hands. Tell the children that each small group is a bubble. Challenge them to "blow" together like a bubble floating around the room. Tell the children they must avoid contact with other bubbles. If they touch another bubble, the two bubbles join together to become a larger bubble. When all the bubbles become one big bubble, the bubble drops to the floor with a loud "pop!" If you play this game outdoors and it is safe, make the game more challenging by having the children close their eyes.

- *Back-to-Back Lift:* Two children sit on the floor back-to-back and lean against each other to stand up. Locking arms may help.

- **Participate in community and school events.**
  - Have a Sidewalk Art Sale and give the proceeds to a favorite charity. Encourage children to create several works of art.
  - Collect food for less fortunate families. Each day, have the children sort and classify the donated food and put it in boxes so it will be ready to transport.
  - Recycle paper products or aluminum cans. Donate the proceeds to a worthy cause.

- **Work on group projects.**
  - Plant a garden. Make sure the group participates in the entire process of preparing the garden, planting the seeds, caring for the plants, and harvesting the vegetables when they are ready. Cook the vegetables and then have a tasting party.
  - Paint a mural. Post a strip of bulletin-board paper on the wall and invite the group to work on a mural. Discuss what the mural will be about before starting. Let each child choose a part that she will be responsible for painting or drawing.
  - Build a house from empty cereal boxes. When you have a good collection of boxes, have the group work together to tape or glue the boxes together to

build a house. Discuss how the boxes have been saved over a period of time. Make sure everyone has a part in designing and building the house.

- Invite the group to select, purchase, and care for a pet. Make sure they select an animal that is appropriate (disease-free, easy to care for, long-living, and high in stamina), such as a hamster or guinea pig.
- Have the group work on a 100-piece puzzle. Let them add pieces each day as they find them. Make sure everyone participates.
- Invite the group to play with a parachute. Point out that it takes everyone holding an edge to lift the parachute into the air.

- **Provide problem-solving scenarios.** Encourage children to work together toward a solution. See pages 32–33 for scenario suggestions.

- **Encourage children's friendships.** Friendships are the beginning of cooperation. Once a child learns to work closely with a friend, she can take what she has learned and apply it to a larger group. See activities to encourage friendships on pages 77–78.

- **Encourage sharing and taking turns.**
  - One reason a child has trouble sharing is because she does not understand that she will be able to get the toy she was playing with back again. To a young child, possession is ownership.
  - Encourage the child to share things that she has multiples of, such as blocks, crayons, or snacks. It can be far easier to share these items because there are many available. Gradually encourage the sharing of single items, such as a doll or a truck. Talk about taking turns so that the child understands that after a time, it will again be her turn. Keep each child's turn fairly short—just a few minutes for young children. A timer works wonders!
  - Give the child some control. For example, if she is playing with two cars and another child wants to play, let her decide which car she will share with her friend. "Which car should Christopher play with, the red one or the black one?"
  - Be sure that the child sees you sharing your time and possessions with others, if possible.

- **Use peer tutoring and the buddy system.** Peer tutoring promotes the highest percentage of retention of learned information. According to David Sousa (2005), information shared during peer tutoring has a 90% chance of being retained.

"We are all dependent on one another, every soul of us on earth."
—George Bernard Shaw

- Invite a language-proficient child to work with children who are less proficient—second-language learners, reluctant speakers, and children with special needs.
- Challenge an older child to teach skills to younger children.

● **Model manners.** See page 74 for suggestions about helping the child practice manners.

Acknowledge Cooperativeness

● **When you see children sharing, taking turns, or being kind to others, let them know that you notice their social skills.** The child is likely to repeat actions that earn her positive feedback.

● **Comment on how work is done easily when several people are helping.** For example, cleaning up or bringing in toys from outside is easier when everyone helps.

● **Notice projects that children organize that require cooperation,** such as building a town or farm, creating a context for play, or digging a tunnel outdoors in the sandbox.

Reflect on Cooperativeness

● **Ask children questions that encourage them to think about cooperation.**
  - Why is cleanup easier when everyone helps?
  - Families share the work that keeps the household thriving. What would happen if one person in a family had to do all the work?
  - How would you feel if someone was helping you put a puzzle together and quit in the middle?
  - What things are more fun to do with a friend?
  - What things are you unable to do by yourself?

Appendix

SONGS, ACTION RHYMES, AND CHANTS RELATED TO SOCIAL AND EMOTIONAL SKILLS

Confidence

Songs

I Like School by Pam Schiller
(Tune: "London Bridge Is Falling Down")

I like to sing with my friends,
With my friends, with my friends.
I like to sing with my friends,
Friends like you.

I like to paint and build with blocks,
Build with blocks, build with blocks.
I like to paint and build with blocks.
I like school, don't you?

I like to move and dance with scarves,
Dance with scarves, dance with
*   scarves.*
I like to move and dance with scarves.
I like school, don't you?

I like to play on the swings and slide,
Swings and slide, swings and slide.
I like to play on the swings and slide.
I like school, don't you?

I like to sing with my friends,
With my friends, with my friends.
I like to sing with my friends,
Friends like you.

This Little Light of Mine
(Traditional)

This little light of mine,
I'm gonna let it shine.
This little light of mine,
I'm gonna let it shine.
This little light of mine,
I'm gonna let it shine.
Let it shine, let it shine,
Let it shine.

Playing with my friends
I'm gonna let it shine.
Playing with my friends
I'm gonna let it shine.
Playing with my friends
I'm gonna let it shine.
Let it shine, let it shine,
Let it shine.

Singing with my mom
I'm gonna let it shine.
Singing with my mom
I'm gonna let it shine.
Singing with my mom
I'm gonna let it shine.
Let it shine, let it shine,
Let it shine.

Create additional verses to match activities that children enjoy.

If You're Clever and You Know It
(adapted by Pam Schiller)

If you're clever and you know it,
Point to a circle.
If you're clever and you know it,
Point to a circle.
If you're clever and you know it,
Then your brain can help you show it.
If you're clever and you know it,
Point to a circle.

Additional verses:
Square
Something red
Something big

Action Rhymes

Five Fingers on Each Hand
(Traditional)

I have five fingers on each hand,
Ten toes on my two feet.
Two ears, two eyes,
One nose, one mouth,
With which to sweetly speak.

My hands can clap, my feet can tap,
My eyes can clearly see.
My ears can hear,
My nose can sniff,
My mouth can say I'm me.

I Can Do It Myself (Traditional)

Hat on head, just like this
Pull it down, you see.
I can put my hat on
All by myself, just me.

One arm in, two arms in,
Buttons, one, two, three.
I can put my coat on
All by myself, just me.

Toes in first, heels down next,
Pull and pull, then see,
I can put my boots on
All by myself, just me.

Fingers here, thumbs right here,
Hands warm as can be.
I can put my mittens on
All by myself, just me.

Chant

I Can, Can You? by Pam Schiller

I can put my hands up high. Can you?
I can wink my eye. Can you?
I can stick out my tongue. Can you?
I can open my mouth wide. Can you?
I can fold my arms. Can you?
I can cover my ears. Can you?
I can touch my nose. Can you?
I can give myself a great big hug. Can
you?
And if I give my hug to you, will you
give me yours, too?

Curiosity

Songs

The Bear Went Over the Mountain
(Traditional)

The bear went over the mountain.
The bear went over the mountain.
The bear went over the mountain
To see what he could see,
To see what he could see,
To see what he could see.
The bear went over the mountain.
The bear went over the mountain.
The bear went over the mountain
To see what he could see.

The other side of the mountain,
The other side of the mountain,
The other side of the mountain
Was all that he could see.
Was all that he could see.
Was all that he could see.
The other side of the mountain,
The other side of the mountain,
The other side of the mountain
Was all that he could see!

Little Skunk's Hole (Traditional)
(Tune: "Dixie")
Oh, I stuck my head
In the little skunk's hole,
And the little skunk said,
"Well, bless my soul!
Take it out! Take it out!
Take it out! Remove it!"

Oh, I didn't take it out,
And the little skunk said,
"If you don't take it out
You'll wish you had.
Take it out! Take it out!"
Pheew! I removed it!

Twinkle, Twinkle Little Star
(Traditional)
Twinkle, twinkle, little star,
How I wonder what you are!
Up above the world so high,
Like a diamond in the sky!
Twinkle, twinkle, little star,
How I wonder what you are!

When the blazing sun is set,
And the grass with dew is wet,
Then you show your little light,
Twinkle, twinkle, all the night.
Twinkle, twinkle, little star,
How I wonder what you are!

In the dark blue sky you keep,
Often through my curtains peep,
For you never shut your eye,
'Til the sun is in the sky.
Twinkle, twinkle, little star,
How I wonder what you are!

Where Is Thumbkin? (Traditional)
Where is Thumbkin? (hands behind
    back)
Where is Thumbkin?
Here I am. Here I am. (bring out right
    thumb, then left)
How are you today, sir? (bend right
    thumb)
Very well, I thank you. (bend left
    thumb)
Run away, run away. (put right
    thumb behind back, then left
    thumb behind back)
Other verses:
Where is Pointer?
Where is Middle One?
Where is Ring Finger?
Where is Pinky?

Action Rhyme

Cloud (Traditional)

What's fluffy white and floats up high
   (point skyward)
Like a pile of cotton in the sky?
And when the wind blows hard and
   strong, (wiggle fingers moving
   horizontally)
What very gently floats along?
   (wiggle fingers moving
   downward)
What brings the rain? (open hands
   palm up)
What brings the snow
That showers down on us below?
When you look up in the high blue sky,
   (look up)
What is that thing you see float by?
   (answer...*a cloud*)

Chant

I Have Something in My Pocket
(Traditional)
I have something in my pocket
It belongs across my face.
I keep it very close at hand
In a most convenient place.

I bet you could guess it,
If you guessed a long, long while,
So I'll take it out and put it on.
It's a great big happy SMILE!

Intentionality

Songs

Itsy Bitsy Spider (Traditional)

The itsy bitsy spider went up the
   waterspout,
Down came the rain and washed the
   spider out.
Up came the sun and dried up all the
   rain.
The itsy bitsy spider went up the
   spout again.

These Are Things I Like to Do
by Pam Schiller
(Tune: "Mary Had a Little Lamb")
These are things I like to do,
Like to do, like to do.
These are things I like to do.
I know a trick or two.

This is the way I read a book,
Read a book, read a book.
This is the way I read a book.
I know a trick or two.

Additional verses:
   I paint a picture...
   I throw the ball...
   I ride my bike...
   I climb a tree...
   I help my dad...

   This is the way we sing our song,
   Sing our song, sing our song.
   This is the way we sing our song.
   We've sung our song, now how 'bout
      you?

Self-Control

Songs

Are You Listening? by Pam Schiller
(Tune: "Are You Sleeping?")
Are you listening?
Are you listening,
Boys and girls, girls and boys?
Come and join our circle.
Come and join our circle.
Sit right down.
Sit right down.

Happy Faces by Pam Schiller
(Tune: "Jingle Bells")
Smiling faces, happy faces,
Giggling all around,
Oh, what fun we'll have today,
As we work and play!
Ha-ha-ha, he-he-he-
Ha-ha-ha, ho-ho-hey!
Oh, what fun we'll have today,
As we work and play!

If You're Happy (Traditional)
(Tune: "If You're Happy and You
Know It")
If you're happy and you know it,
*   laugh out loud. (ha, ha, ha)*
If you're happy and you know it,
*   laugh out loud. (ha, ha, ha)*
If you're happy and you know it,
Then your laugh can help you show it
If you're happy and you know it,
*   laugh out loud. (ha, ha, ha)*

If you're sad and you know it, say, "I'm
*   sad." ("I'm sad!")*
If you're sad and you know it, say, "I'm
*   sad." ("I'm sad!")*

If you're sad and you know it,
Then your words can help you show it
If you're sad and you know it, say, "I'm
*   sad."("I'm sad!")*

If you're angry and you know it,
*   stomp your feet. (stomp, stomp,*
*   stomp)*
If you're angry and you know it,
*   stomp your feet. (stomp, stomp,*
*   stomp)*
If you're angry and you know it,
Then your feet can help you show it.
If you're angry and you know it,
*   stomp your feet. (stomp, stomp,*
*   stomp)*

If you're surprised and you know it,
*   say, "yippee!" ("yippee!")*
If you're surprised and you know it,
*   say, "yippee!" ("yippee!")*
If you're surprised and you know it,
Then your words can help you show it,
If you're surprised and you know it,
*   say, "yippee!" ("yippee!")*

S-M-I-L-E (Traditional)
(Tune: "Battle Hymn of the Republic")
It isn't any trouble
Just to S-M-I-L-E.
It isn't any trouble
Just to S-M-I-L-E.
So smile when you're in trouble,
It will vanish like a bubble
If you'll only take the trouble
Just to S-M-I-L-E!

It isn't any trouble
Just to L-A-U-G-H. (or ha-ha-ha-ha
*   laugh)*

It isn't any trouble
Just to L-A-U-G-H. (or ha-ha-ha-ha
    laugh)
So laugh when you're in trouble,
It will vanish like a bubble
If you'll only take the trouble
Just to L-A-U-G-H! (or ha-ha-ha-ha
    laugh)

It isn't any trouble
Just to G-R-I-N, grin.
It isn't any trouble
Just to G-R-I-N, grin.
So grin when you're in trouble
It will vanish like a bubble
If you'll only take the trouble
Just to G-R-I-N, grin!

Ha! Ha! Ha! Ha! Ha! Ha!
Ha! Ha! Ha! Ha! Ha! Ha! Ha!
Ha! Ha! Ha! Ha! Ha! Ha!
Ha! Ha! Ha! Ha! Ha! Ha! Ha!
Ha! Ha! Ha! Ha! Ha! Ha!
Ha! Ha! Ha! Ha! Ha! Ha! Ha!
Ha! Ha! Ha! Ha! Ha! Ha! Ha! Ha! Ha!

Stop, Drop, and Roll (Traditional)
(Tune: "Hot Cross Buns")
Stop, drop, and roll.
Stop, drop, and roll.
If ever your clothes catch on fire,
Stop, drop, and roll.

Remember this rule,
This golden safety rule.
If ever your clothes catch on fire,
Stop, drop, and roll.

Action Rhymes
I Wiggle My Fingers (Traditional)
(suit actions to words)
I wiggle my fingers.
I wiggle my toes.
I wiggle my shoulders.
I wiggle my nose.
Now no more wiggles are left in me.
So I can sit still as I can be.

Open, Shut Them (Traditional)
Open, shut them, open, shut them.
Give a little clap, clap, clap.
Open, shut them, open, shut them.
Place them in your lap.
Creep them, creep them,
Creep them, creep them,
Right up to your chin.
Open wide your little mouth,
But do not let them in.
Open, shut them, open, shut them
Give a little clap, clap, clap.
Open, shut them, open, shut them.
Place them in your lap.

Quiet Time (Traditional)
Let your hands go clap, clap, clap.
    (clap)
Let your feet go tap, tap, tap. (tap)
Fold your hands in you lap. (put
    hands in lap)
*Don't go to sleep—It's not time to
    nap.* (shake head no)
Do you know what time it is?
    (answer: *Quiet Time*)

Chants

Be Very Quiet (Traditional)

Shhh, be very quiet,
Shhh, be very still.
Fold your busy little hands,
Close your sleepy little eyes.
Shhh, be very quiet.

Stop, Look, and Listen (Traditional)

Stop, look, and listen
Before you cross the street.
First use your eyes and ears,
Then use your feet.

Who Took the Cookies?

(Traditional)

Who took the cookies from the
*   cookie jar?*
Evan took the cookies from the
*   cookie jar.*
Who me?
Yes, you.
Couldn't be.
Then who?
Madison took the cookies from the
*   cookie jar.*
Who me?
Yes, you.
Couldn't be.
Then who?
(Continue the chant with other
children and end with "Daddy took
the cookies from the cookie jar.")
That's who!

Relating to Others

Songs

For He's a Jolly Good Fellow

(Traditional)

For he's a jolly good fellow,
For he's a jolly good fellow,
For he's a jolly good fellow,
Which nobody can deny.
Which nobody can deny.
Which nobody can deny.
For he's a jolly good fellow,
For he's a jolly good fellow,
For he's a jolly good fellow,
Which nobody can deny.

We won't go home until morning
We won't go home until morning
We won't go home until morning
Till daylight doth appear
Till daylight doth appear
Till daylight doth appear
We won't go home until morning
We won't go home until morning
We won't go home until morning
Till daylight doth appear

Hello, Good Friend (Traditional)

(Tune: "Are You Sleeping?")
Hello, good friend
Hello, good friend.
How are you?
How are you?
Say your name to us friend,
Say your name to us friend.
And we will clap for you.
We'll clap for you.

Make New Friends (Traditional)

Make new friends,
But keep the old.
One is silver,
And the other's gold.
(Repeat twice)

The More We Get Together
(Traditional)

The more we get together, together,
*   together.*
The more we get together, the happier
*   we'll be.*
For your friends are my friends
And my friends are your friends.
The more we get together, the happier
*   we'll be.*

One Elephant (Traditional)

One elephant went out to play.
Out on a spider's web one day.
He had such enormous fun,
He called for another elephant to
*   come.*

Children sit in a circle. One child walks around in a circle with one arm stretched out in front to make a trunk, while the group sings the song. When the lyrics "called for another elephant to come" are sung, the child chooses a friend to join him. The game continues until all children are chosen to be elephants at play. Best played with a group of 3 or 4 children.

Say, Say My Playmate (Traditional)

Say, say my playmate,
Come out and play with me.

And bring your dollies three.
Climb up my apple tree.
Look down my rain barrel.
Slide down my cellar door.
And we'll be jolly friends,
Forever more.

It was a really rainy day,
And she couldn't come
Out to play.
With tearful eyes
And tender sighs,
I could hear her say:
I'm sorry playmate.
I cannot play with you.
My dollies have the flu.
Boo-hoo hoo hoo hoo hoo.
Can't climb your rain barrel.
Can't slide your cellar door.
But we'll be jolly friends,
Forever more.

Skidamarink (Traditional)

Skidamarink a dink a dink,
Skidamarink a doo,
I love you.
Skidamarink a dink a dink,
Skidamarink a doo,
I love you.

I love you in the morning
And in the afternoon,
I love you in the evening
And underneath the moon;
Oh, Skidamarink a dink a dink,
Skidamarink a doo,
I love you!

This Is Quinn by Pam Schiller
(Tune: "Here We Go Round the
Mulberry Bush")
(Substitute names and
characteristics to individualize the
song)
Here is our friend
His name is Quinn,
His name is Quinn,
His name is Quinn.
Here is our friend
We're glad he's here
Say "hello" to Quinn.

This Is Tiffany by Pam Schiller
(Tune: "Six White Ducks")
This is Tiffany over here.
She has on a bright blue dress.
This is Tiffany, our new friend.
We're so glad she's here.

This is Patrick over here.
He has on new black shoes.
This is Patrick, our new friend.
We're so glad he's here.

This is Carmen over here.
She has on a fuzzy pink sweater.
This is Carmen, our new friend.
We're so glad she's here.

This is Jonathan over here.
He has on his favorite red shirt.
This is Jonathan, our new friend.
We're so glad he's here.

What Goes Together? by Pam
Schiller
(Tune: "Itsy Bitsy Spider")
What goes together?
A button and a coat.
What goes together?
Grass and a goat.
What goes together?
A dog and a flea.
Putting things together,
Good friends like you and me.
(Repeat)

Action Rhyme

Five Little Ladybugs by Pam
Schiller and Richele Bartkowiak
(Begin with five fingers up— put one
down each time a ladybug leaves—
bring all five fingers back at the end.)
Five little ladybugs dancing on the
*   shore,*
One danced away and then there were
*   four*
Four little ladybugs dipping in the sea
One chased a fish and then there were
*   three.*
Three little lady bugs admiring the
*   view*
One skipped off and then there were
*   two,*
Two little ladybugs bathing in the sun
One flew home leaving only one.
One little ladybug all alone.
She called her friends on the
*   telephone.*
They came back, now there's five
To dance and sing the ladybug jive!

Chants

Good Morning to You! (Traditional, adapted by Pam Schiller)

Good morning to you!
Good morning to you!
We're all in our places
With bright, shining faces,
This is the way to start a great day!

Good afternoon to you!
Good afternoon to you!
We're all in our places
With food on our faces,
This is the way to have a great day!

Good evening to you!
Good evening to you!
Stars and moon in their places,
Shine light on our faces.
This is the way to end a great day!

Hello, Hello (Traditional)

Hello, hello, hello, hello!
We are glad to meet you.
We are glad to greet you.
Hello, hello, hello, hello!

Nobody Likes Me *(Traditional)*

Nobody likes me, everybody hates me,
Guess I'll go eat worms,
Long, thin, slimy ones; Short, fat, juicy ones,
Itsy, bitsy, fuzzy wuzzy worms.

Down goes the first one, down goes the second one,
Oh how they wiggle and squirm.
Up comes the first one, up comes the second one,

Oh how they wiggle and squirm.

Nobody likes me, everybody hates me,
Think I'll go eat worms.
Big fat juicy ones, little slimy skinny ones,
Hope they don't have germs!

Communication

Songs

Catalina Magnalina (Traditional)

She had a peculiar name but she
  wasn't to blame,
She got it from her mother who's the
  same, same, same.

Chorus: Catalina, Magnalina,
  Hootensteiner, Bogentwiner,
  Hogan, Logan, Bogan, was her
  name.

She had two peculiar teeth in her
  mouth
One pointed north and the other
  pointed south.
(Chorus)
She had two peculiar eyes in her head,
One was purple and the other was
  red.
(Chorus)
She had two peculiar hairs on her
  chin,
One stuck out and the other stuck in.
(Chorus)
Her feet were as flat as a bathroom
  mat,
I forgot to ask her how they got like
  that.
(Chorus)

Sing a Song of Signs by Pam Schiller
(Tune: "Mary Had a Little Lamb")
This is please and this is thank you.
This is please; this is thank you.
This is please and this is thank you.
Sign along with me.

Please

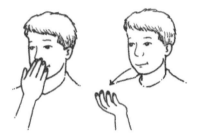

Thank You

Additional verses:
This is more and this is stop....
This is up and this is down....
This is sad and this is happy....

This Old Man (Traditional, variation
by Pam Schiller)
This Old Man, he played drums
With his fingers and his thumbs.

Chorus:
With a nick-nack paddy whack give a
*   dog a bone*
This Old Man is rockin' on.

This Old Man, he played flute,
Made it hum and made it toot.
(Chorus)
This Old Man, he played strings,
Twangs and twops and zips and zings.
(Chorus)
This Old Man, he played bass,
With a big grin on his face.
(Chorus)
This Old Man, he played gong
At the end of every song.
(Chorus)
This Old Man, he could dance.
He could strut and he could prance.
(Chorus)
This Old Man was a band,
Very best band in the land.
(Chorus)

Cooperation

Songs

Calliope Song (Traditional)
Sound 1: *Um pa pa, um pa pa...*
Sound 2: *Um tweedli-dee, um tweedli-*
    dee...
Sound 3: *Um shhh ,um shhh, um*
    shhh...
Divide children into four groups.
Instruct group one to make sound 1,
group two to make sound 2, and
group three to make sound 3.
Group four will hum the circus song
(the merry-go-round song).

Can You Put the Toys Away? by
Pam Schiller
(Tune: "Oh, Do You Know the Muffin
Man?")
Oh, can you put the toys away, toys
away, toys away?
Oh, can you put the toys away?
It's time to end our play.
(Repeat)

Clean Up (Traditional)
Clean up! Clean up!
Everybody, everywhere.
Clean up! Clean up!
Everybody, do your share.

Action Rhyme
I Help My Family by Pam Schiller
(suit actions to words)
I help my family when I can.
I fold the clothes.
I feed the dog.
I turn on the hose.

I crack the eggs.
I ice the cake.
Then I help eat
The good things we make.

Chant
I'm a Family Helper by Pam Schiller
I set the table every night
I learned to do it right.
One place for mom, one for me,
And Daddy's place makes three.

I pick my toys up everyday,
I put everything away.
My cars, my blocks, my books
All go into their nooks.

A family helper is what I am
You can be one, too.
Mommy say's I m quite a ham
When it comes to jobs I do.

RECIPES

Gak

2 cups glue
1½ cups tap water
2 teaspoons Borax
1 cup hot water
food coloring

Combine glue, tap water, and food coloring in a bowl. In a larger bowl, dissolve Borax in hot water. Slowly add glue mixture to Borax. It will thicken quickly and be difficult to mix. Mix well and drain off excess water. Let the mixture stand for a few minutes then pour into a shallow tray. Let it dry for 10 minutes. Store in a re-sealable plastic bag. (It will keep for 2–3 weeks.)

Goop

2 cups salt
1 cup water
1 cup cornstarch

Cook salt and ½ cup water for 4–5 minutes. Remove from heat. Add cornstarch and ½ cup water. Return to heat. Stir until mixture thickens. Store in a resealable plastic bag or covered container.

Partner Ice Cream

Mix ½ cup milk, 1 tablespoon sugar, and ¼ teaspoon vanilla in a 1-pound clean coffee can. Place the 1-pound can inside a 5-pound can and fill with ice and salt. Give the can to two children and have them roll it back and forth to one another until they no longer hear the slush of the mixture inside. Open the can and allow the children to share the ice cream.

SOCIAL AND EMOTIONAL SKILLS MATRIX

Characteristic	Emerging	Mastery
Confidence	Participates in routines.	Participates in new experiences with ease. For example, asks questions.
	Identifies a problem. For example, the puzzle is missing a piece.	Attempts to solve problems. For example, "The puzzle is missing a piece. Can we make a new piece?"
	Attempts new activities with adult support. For example, asks for help to ride a bike.	Approaches new activities without adult support. For example, begins to play with the bike.
	Expresses an awareness of self in terms of physical characteristics.	Expresses an awareness of self in terms of abilities and preferences.
	Demonstrates independence in routines.	Demonstrates independence in activities and tasks.
	Expresses joy in accomplishments.	Expresses pride in accomplishments.
Curiosity	Asks questions.	Asks questions and seeks answers.
	Demonstrates interest in new items in the room.	Explores and ask questions about new items in the room.
	Notices unfamiliar objects. For example, picks up and examines a clock that picks up and examines a clock that is new. Notices similarities and differences in materials when they are pointed out by someone else.	Shows interest in investigating unfamiliar objects. For example, asks how the new clock works. Compares objects and organisms by similarities and differences. For example, "These rocks are like chalk."
	Listens to a story from beginning to end.	Shows desire to know what will happen next in a story.
	Discusses which things in the story could really happen and which things could not really happen.	Participates in thinking of ways the story would change if one of the characters or events in the story were to change.
	Participates in art projects that are open-ended. For example, paints at the easel, sponge paints, draws objects of her own choice.	Shows imagination in artwork. For example, uses two different media to complete his work, turns the paper a different direction when drawing.

Characteristic	Emerging	Mastery
Intentionality	Makes choices with assistance.	Makes choices with limited options without assistance.
	Finishes activities with adult support.	Finishes activities without reminders or assistance.
	Articulates choices.	Articulates choices and explains rationale behind his choices. For example, "I am working with markers because I want to make a picture for my sister."
	Finishes chosen activities.	Sticks with projects that develop over time.
Self-Control	Follows rules with reminders.	Follows rules without reminders.
	Responds to guidance from adults.	Responds to guidance from an adult by changing future behavior.
	Expresses feelings, needs, and opinions.	Expresses feeling, needs, and opinions in difficult situations without aggression.
	Treats materials respectfully with guidance from an adult.	Treats materials respectfully.
	Manages routines.	Adapts to changes in routines.
	Recognizes the effect of his behavior on others.	Regulates behavior that will result in negative responses from others.
	Recognizes emotions and labels them.	Attempts to regulate and manage emotions.
	Participates in resolution of social conflicts with adult guidance.	Attempts to solve social conflicts independent of adult intervention.
Relating to Others	Recognizes likenesses and differences among peers. For example, "Yin is younger than I am. Tamiko uses a wheelchair to move around."	Accepts likenesses and differences among peers. For example, attempts to help a younger child or invites a child in a wheelchair to play ball.
	Takes turns in games.	Attempts to take turns and share. For example, tells a friend that he can share a truck by each driving it one way on a back and forth trip to the farm.

Characteristic	Emerging	Mastery
Relating to Others (continued)	Shows interest in developing friendships. For example, plays beside children and copies their actions.	Sustains friendships with one or two friends. For example, selects the same child to play with over a period of time.
	Shows awareness of other's feelings. For example, says, "That boy is sad."	Demonstrates empathy by responding to concerns of others. For example, helps a peer who falls down or sits by a child who is having a bad day.
	Accepts a role suggested by an adult when joining a group.	Joins in group play by finding a place for herself. For example, "I can be the teacher."
	Accepts guidance from familiar adults.	Accepts guidance from a variety of adults—familiar and unfamiliar.
Capacity to Communicate	Makes basic wants and needs known. For example, needing to use the bathroom, feeling hunger.	Stands up for himself. For example, says "no" when a peer attempts to take his toy.
	Describes herself using simple attributes. For example, uses the terms "girl," "tall," "fast."	Describes himself and others using comparisons. For example, "We're wearing red."
	Expresses fears and concerns to an adult. For example, "I don't like rabbits."	Manages fears and concerns with adult support. For example, asks an adult to hold her hand when fearful.
	Interacts with familiar adults when adults initiate interaction. For example, responds to adult directions, answers, and questions when asked.	Engages in conversations with familiar adults, asks questions, follows directions, and often initiates conversation.
	Uses verbal etiquette when prompted.	Uses verbal etiquette without being prompted.
	Enjoys playing with rhyming words and alliterations.	Identifies rhyming words and alliterations.
Cooperativeness	Attempts to join play of the group by occasional talking to members in the group.	Plays cooperatively with one or two friends.
	Participates in group play.	Suggests ideas for group play. For example, "Let's play zookeeper and each be a different animal."
	Participates in clean-up time.	Recognizes that clean-up time and other activities are easier when everyone does their share.

Conversation Starter Cards

If you had to give up one of these foods for the rest of your life, which one would you give up: cookies, French fries, or chicken nuggets?	If you were a clown, what color hair would you have?	Which one of these weather words best describes the way you feel today: sunny, cloudy, windy, stormy, calm?
Do you like daytime or nighttime better? Why?	Which shape do you like best— a circle, a square, or a triangle? Why?	If you opened a toy store, what toys would you sell in your store?
If you had a special secret box, what would you put in it?	What do you think milk would taste like if it were green instead of white?	Which day of the week is your favorite? Why?
If you could have one characteristic of a zoo animal, what would it be?	Which bird do you think looks funnier, an ostrich or a pelican?	What sound, other than ringing, would you want a doorbell to make?
If you could design a playground, what would it look like?	If you could change the shape of the windows on your car, what shape would you want them to be?	Which goat in the story of "The Three Billy Goats Gruff" would you want to be? Why?

REFERENCES AND RESOURCES

Bailey, B. 2004. *Conscious Discipline Live* DVD. Jacksonville, Florida: Loving Guidance.

Bandura, A. 1986. *Social foundations of thought and action: A social cognitive.* Englewood Cliffs, NJ: Prentice Hall.

Bandura, A. 2000. Self-efficacy. In A. E. Kazdin (Ed.), *Encyclopedia of Psychology.* New York: Oxford University Press.

Barnes, B. & S. York. 2001. *Common sense parenting of toddlers and preschoolers.* Boystown, NV: Boys Town Press.

Blimes, J. 2008. *Beyond behavior management.* St. Paul, MN: Redleaf Press.

Bower, B. 2005. *Science News* 167(18): 278-278 (April 2005).

Bransford, J., A. Brown, & R. Cocking, (Eds.). 1999. *How people learn: Brain, mind, experience, and school.* Washington, DC: National Academy Press.

Bredekamp, S., & Cl. Copple. 1997. *Developmentally appropriate practices in the early childhood classroom, revised edition.* Washington, DC: National Association for the Education of Young Children (NAEYC).

Bredekamp, S., & T. Rosegrant. 1995. Reaching potentials through national standards: Panacea or pipe dream? In S. Bredekamp & T. Rosegrant (Eds.). *Reaching potentials: Transforming early childhood curriculum and assessment.* Washington, DC: National Association for the Education of Young Children (NAEYC).

Brooks, D. 2006. Self-control is the key to success. *New York Times*, May 9.

Bruner, J. 1996. *The culture of education.* Cambridge, MA: Harvard University Press.

Caine, R.N., & G. Caine. 1994. *Making connections: Teaching and the human brain.* Menlo Park, CA: Addison-Wesley.

Caine, R., G. Caine, C. McClintic, & K. Klimek. 2008. *The 12 Brain/Mind Learning Principles in Action,* 2nd edition, Thousand Oaks, CA: Corwin Press.

Clark, D. L., & T. A. Astuto. Redirecting reform: Challenges to popular assumptions about teachers and students. *Phi Delta Kappan*: 513-520 (March 1994).

Danner, F., & E. Lonky. 1981. A cognitive-developmental approach to the effects of rewards on intrinsic motivation. *Child Development* 52: 1050.

Dreikurs, R., P. Cassel, & E. Dreikurs-Ferguson. 2004. *Discipline without tears: How to reduce conflict and establish cooperation in the classroom.* Hoboken, NJ: Wiley.

Dreikurs, R., B. Grunwald, & F. Pepper. 1998. *Maintaining sanity in the classroom: Classroom management techniques.* New York: Taylor & Francis.

Epstein, A. 2007. *The intentional teacher*. Washington, DC: National Association for the Education of Young Children (NAEYC).

Families and Work Institute. 1996. *Rethinking the brain: New insights into early development*. Executive Summary of the Conference on Brain Development in Young Children: New Frontiers for Research, Policy, and Practice, University of Chicago, June.

Gamon, D., & A. Bragdon. 2003. *Building mental muscle.* New York: Walker & Company.

Glossop, R. & A. Mitchell.2005. "Heart smarts." Contemporary Family Trends (November 2005). Ontario, Canada: The Vanier Institute of the Family.

Goleman, D. 1995. *Emotional intelligence: Why it can matter more than IQ.* New York: Bantam Books.

Goleman, D. 2007. *Social intelligence: The new science of human relationships.* New York: Bantam Books.

Gurian, M. 2007. *Nurture the nature.* San Francisco, CA: Jossey-Bass.

Hannaford, C. 1995. *Smart moves: Why learning is not all in your head.* Arlington, VA: Great Ocean Publishers.

Healy, J. M. 1999. *Endangered minds.* New York: Simon & Schuster.

Healy, J. M. 1987. *Your child's growing mind.* New York: Doubleday.

Helm, J. 2009. "Best Brains in Science Under Five: Helping Children Develop Intentionality." *Child Care Information Exchange* 31, no. 1.

Irons, K.R. Comment on The Parents Blog. http://parenting.families.com/blog/eitheror-choices-for-children/ (posted May 20, 2007).

Iyengar, S., & M. Lepper. 2000. When choice is demotivating: Can one desire too much of a good thing? *Journal of Personality and Social Psychology* 79: 995-1006.

Jensen, E. 1998. T*eaching with the brain in mind.* Alexandria, VA: Association for Supervision and Curriculum Development.

Jensen, E. 2005. *Teaching with the brain in mind,* revised 2nd edition. Alexandria, VA: Association for Supervision and Curriculum Development.

Jowles, J. 2004. Cognitive performance and learning, related to motivation, psychosocial and emotional Factors. Position paper for the conference on Emotion, Learning and Education. Copenhagan.

Juvonen, J., & K.R. Wentzel. 1996. *Social motivation: Understanding children's school adjustment.* New York: Cambridge University Press.

Kines, B. Too many choices can be frustrating to children. *Teaching Pre K-8* (January 1998).

Kohn, A. *Children and choices.* Phi Delta Kappan (September 1993).

Kohn, A. Five reasons to stop saying 'Good job'. *Young Children 56,* (5): 24-28 (2001).

Lewis, C., E. Schaps, & M. Watson. The caring classrooms' academic edge. *Educational Leadership:* 16-21 (September 1996).

Mitchell, A. & Glossop, R. *Heart smarts. Contemporary Family Trends:* (Autumn 2005). The Vanier Institute of the Family: Ottowa, Canada.

Morrison, G.S. 1997. *Fundamentals of early childhood education.* Upper Saddle River, NJ: Merrill/Prentice Hall.

Nash, M. 1997. Fertile minds. *Time,* February.

Newmann, F. M. Beyond common sense in educational restructuring: The issues of content and linkage. *Educational Researcher* 22 (20): 4-13, 22 (1993).

Paley, V. 1999. *The kindness of children.* Cambridge, MA: Harvard University Press.

Perry, B. D., L. Hogan, & S. Marlin. 2000. Curiosity, pleasure and play: A neurodevelopmental perspective. Houston, TX: HAAEYC Advocate. Perry, B. 2001. Curiosity: The fuel of development. *Early Childhood Today.* New York: Scholastic.

Ramey, C., & S. Ramey. 1999. *Right from birth: Building your child's foundation For Life.* New York: Goddard Press.

Ratcliff, N. Use the environment to prevent discipline problems and support learning. *Young Children 56* (5): 84-87 (2001).

Schiller, P. 1999. *Start smart: Building brain power in the early years.* Beltsville, MD: Gryphon House.

Schiller, P. & T. Bryant. 1998. *The values book.* Beltsville, MD: Gryphon House.

ScienceDaily. 2006, August 27: Pure novelty spurs the brain. Cell Press. www.sciencedaily.com.

Shoda, Y., W. Mischel, & P.K. Peake. Predicting adolescent cognitive and self-regulatory competencies from preschool delay of gratification: Identifying diagnostic conditions. *Developmental Psychology* 26 (6): 978–986 (1990).

Siegel, D. 1999. *The developing mind.* New York: Guilford Press.

Snow, C. 2005. "From Literacy to Learning." Harvard Education Letter (July/August). Online:www.edletter.org/current/snow.shtml.

Sousa, D. A. 2005. *How the brain learns,* 3rd edition. Thousand Oaks, CA: Corwin Press.

Spaulding, C.L. 1992. Motivation in the classroom. New York: McGraw-Hill.

Sylwester, R. 1995. A celebration of neurons: An educator's guide to the human brain. Alexandria, VA: Association for Supervision and Curriculum Development.

Szanton, E. S. 1992. *Heart start: The emotional foundations of school Readiness.* Arlington, VA: National Center for Clinical Infant Programs.

RESOURCES

Common Sense Parenting of Toddlers & Preschoolers by Bridget Barnes and Steven York

Conscious Discipline by Becky Bailey

*Polite Kids 101 DVD: Social Skills Your
    Child Needs For Success In Life!*
    (Production 101, Inc.)
Second Step: A Violence Program
    (Committee for Children)
Simple Signing with Young Children by
    Carol Garboden Murray (Gryphon
    House)
The Share and Get Along Series by Cheri
    Meiners (set of 14 books with
    interactive CDs)
The Values Book (Gryphon House)
You and Me Social Skills Program
    (Wright Group/McGraw-Hill)

WEBSITES
http://www.6seconds.org
http://www.cfchildren.org
http://www.iamyourchild.org
http://www.naeyc.org
http://www.nccic.org
http://www.talaris.org
http://www.zerotothree.org
http://guide.helpingamericasyouth.gov

INDEX

SEVEN SKILLS FOR SCHOOL SUCCESS